# 태권도

한국어의 언어과 용어 참고 도서

밀느스 벤자민 티

# Taekwondo

## A Korean Language and Terminology Reference

Benjamin T. Milnes

First Edition 2009 CE, ISBN 978-1-4452-3105-1

Published by
Lulu Enterprises Inc.

Printed in the United States of America, North Carolina, Raleigh by
Lulu Press Inc.

Copyright © Holder
Benjamin T. Milnes

All rights reserved. This publication may not be fully or partially reproduced in any form or by any means, be it graphic, electronic, mechanical or any other, including photocopying, recording, taping, or any other without prior permission in writing from the copyright holder.

Author and Researcher
Benjamin T. Milnes

Front Cover
King Sejong the Great, Gwanghwamun Square in Gyeongbokgung Palace,
Seoul, South Korea

# 태권도

## 한국어의 언어과 용어 참고도서

밀느스 벤자민 티

# Taekwondo

## A Korean Language and Terminology Reference

Benjamin T. Milnes

# 일
# 서론

# ① Introduction

# Problems with Terminology in Taekwondo

It has become increasingly difficult to be sure what is actually correct information in Taekwondo now. A swift search on the internet will give one hundreds of variations on the same information. With regards to Korean terminology, it has been rewritten so many different times in phonetic script that in some cases the words are completely unrecognisable from their original Korean pronunciation and spelling. Along with this, some words get swapped around, and others get completely made up.

I believe that the cause of this has its roots right back in the division of Taekwondo, when the two titanic organisations split to become the international and world federations. Since then it seems almost normal that once a student reaches a high enough level, to get together with some other like-minded students and create their own organisation of which they are the leaders.

Of course, every time a new organisation is created, documents need to be written for its inauguration, including syllabuses and vocabulary lists. Nobody has the same ideas about how to pronounce new words written in English. Because this segregation means that the new leaders can alter the phonetic script to how they prefer to pronounce it, the language becomes more and more fake each time this separation happens. Many people will also consider the terminology aspect unimportant; hence vocabulary lists may be rushed, which causes yet more problems.

Interestingly, since the instigation of the internet, numerous vocabulary lists have cropped up from different people, each slightly different, some with a few more words than others. As there is no definitive list, groups appear to be sharing these few extra words, which seem to have materialised out of cyberspace.

Therefore we are now left in a situation where some organisations that are the end point of a long series of break-away groups are not speaking Korean at all. At the end of this book I have included a short section of some of the most distorted phrases I found.

Sadly, the terminology is not the only aspect that gets diluted each time a new association appears. Much of the Korean culture and attitude gets lost as well, I thoroughly suggest that you browse the internet and see some of the schools which are barely practising martial arts, and are instead plastering the little remaining information they have with whatever films and television can tell them.

# Intentions and Functions of this Textbook

Hopefully this book will resolve some of the issues and be a reliable list of terminology. In order to ensure its reliability for everyone it will require extra effort from all students in all schools, because I can guarantee now, that there will be many schools out there who are teaching language skills which are just plain wrong, incorrect, and false.

Accompanying this book is an audio disc that reads extracts from the book aloud so that they can be learnt more easily. Parts of this CD are similar to a textbook, listing information or discussing points; this information tends not to need memorising, but is general interest. Other parts are similar to an exercise book, practising and memorising important information that will be needed during lessons or exams.

You can take learning Korean to whatever level you choose. Some prefer to just memorise the words, in which case a reliable source such as this is important. Or you can choose to read around the subject and take on additional elements, such as mastering the symbols.

For lower grades this book can be considered as a course, which you progress along over a few weeks and take in all the information, or as an index, which you might use on occasion as an ultimate source in researching terminology. There is a lot of additional information in this book and you will find varying degrees of relevance. Do not think that you are required to read the entire book in order to understand it.

For higher grades though, it is more important that you read and study most or all information in this book more thoroughly, as you are expected to have a wide knowledge of your martial art.

# Importance and Reasons for Learning Terminology

In any credible martial arts school or club, emphasis is placed not just upon learning the movements of the martial art themselves, but their names and properties. Movements are then organised into complex sequences, or other exercises, to help train the student, and a large section of the syllabus is built up as so. Equally, words and phrases used for describing the movements should be learnt in the language of the martial art's origin country, and the history and culture of that country should also be studied to bring the pupil a significant part of their martial arts education. It is essential in any martial arts school not just to study the practical element, but the theoretical aspects also.

But why is this? Would it not be easier simply to study the movements and focus all concentration on those? If one were training for a competition, then yes it would be a lot more efficient. However, it is becoming increasingly crucial for theoretical parts to be considered.

Firstly, there is the obvious reason that without fixed and proper terminology in at least one language, it would become very difficult to discuss the martial art without a high degree of ambiguity, as people would inherently use their own words to express movements, ensuing confusion. There are many different variants of English terms. Discussion of martial arts movements is vital, particularly for those arts which are not so old, including Taekwondo, which have not had millennia to evolve in. They still require adjustments so that they can reach their full capacity. Without debating these, progress could not be made effectively.

Communicating the movements with strict terminology is of course essential for creating syllabuses. Ambiguity would inevitably mean some practitioners perform the wrong movements by accident.

This standardisation of terms continues to be important when martial artists from different regions get together for an event. Martial arts are commonly known to vary even from club to club, with different techniques being taught, even if the clubs belong to the same organisation. So if we are dealing with international events, then it is imperative that we can all interpret each others phrasing.

Secondly, it adds another layer to any examination procedure. For example, there may be two students, both equally keen on the martial art they are studying, but one may be better at the movements. In a grading this looks as though one is more enthusiastic than the other. Everybody has strengths and weaknesses in different fields, so those who struggle with the physical tasks may excel in other areas, such as language. Studying theoretical aspects provides an opportunity for some to demonstrate their interest in a martial art despite a drawback.

This becomes most useful when the elderly or disabled wish to study the martial art. Some cannot perform the movements, yet through their eagerness and attitude deserve the opportunity to participate in the art. Theoretical study is one means by which this can be done. I know that in many larger organisations, special examinations are provided so that anyone incapable of doing the physical assessment can proceed through the ranks.

Thirdly, and in my own opinion more importantly, martial arts are dangerous knowledge. Any martial arts student must have the highest level of discipline, in order to utilise their proficiency in a virtuous manner. If martial arts were approached with the mindset *"I just want to learn to beat people up!"*, and I have met some who think this, then clearly the moral grounding is absent, and the person should not be granted access to the martial arts knowledge. They could potentially do harm. As martial arts spread across the world, the oriental influence of integrity is weakening. By making terminology and language part of the curriculum, those students who have integrity will recognise the values of self discipline and self control needed to learn the theory, thus they will progress. This setup will deter violent people, who will only want to focus on their aggression and ignore the theory, and will consequently not be able to progress.

Taekwondo belongs to Korea and to the Korean people, as that is its origin country, and it could be viewed as greedy to not want any association with their culture, language, or history and just to want to know how to fuel aggression. Learning the language is absorbing part of another civilization, and in doing so respecting its members and culture. It shows a greater commitment to the martial art and demonstrates an understanding of what it is to study one.

Conclusively, it is just as important to learn the theoretical as well as the practical facet to Taekwondo.

# Contents

The main bulk of this book is reserved for explanation of the terms used in Taekwondo, however they are not arranged by grade because that would associate the book to a particular association, rendering it less useful for members of other organisations. This way, if you want to specifically learn material for your syllabus, you can locate it easily.

Those sections which have a single * asterisk symbol marked by them are fundamental and essential and the minimum amount of information needed to understand the main index. Those which have a double ** asterisk are considered more advanced to allow you full comprehension of the material. The more asterisks there are, the less vital it is to read a certain section.

You will also see as you read the book, the + plus symbol, denoting that there is a special point being made about the information, or alerting you to watch out for a specific idea.

| | | |
|---|---|---|
| ① **INTRODUCTION** | | **7 - 16** |
| | PROBLEMS WITH TERMINOLOGY IN TAEKWONDO ** | 8 - 9 |
| | INTENTIONS AND FUNCTIONS OF THIS TEXTBOOK * | 9 |
| | IMPORANTANCE AND REASONS FOR LEARNING TERMINOLOGY ** | 10 - 11 |
| | CONTENTS | 12 - 15 |
| ② **ORIGINS AND HISTORY** | | **17 - 22** |
| | OVERVIEW *** | 18 |
| | HANJA *** | 18 - 19 |
| | HANGEUL *** | 20 - 22 |
| ③ **LANGUAGE SKILLS AND CONCEPTS** | | **23 - 54** |

| | |
|---|---|
| SOUNDS AND PRONUNCIATION | 24 - 29 |
| VOWELS * | 24 - 26 |
| CONSONANTS * | 26 - 29 |
| CHARACTERS | 29 - 39 |
| COMPONENTS ** | 29 - 34 |
| SYLLABLES ** | 34 - 37 |
| ALPHABETICAL ORDERS *** | 37 - 39 |
| ROMANISATION | 39 - 45 |
| MCCUNE-REISCHAUER AND YALE *** | 39 - 40 |
| REVISED SYSTEM & OUR SYSTEM * | 41 - 45 |
| SIMPLE GRAMMAR | 45 - 50 |
| SENTENCE STRUCTURE *** | 45 - 46 |
| CASE PARTICLES *** | 46 - 47 |
| VERB CONJUGATION AND MODIFICATION *** | 47 |
| FORMALITY AND RESPECT *** | 47 - 50 |
| SUFFIXES AND INFIXES | 50 - 54 |
| DEDUCTIVE REASONING *** | 50 - 51 |
| REGULAR FORMATION *** | 51 - 53 |
| IRREGULAR FORMATION *** | 53 - 54 |
| TRANSLATING NAMES *** | 54 |
| ④ **TERMINOLOGY AND PHRASES** | **55 - 118** |

| | |
|---|---|
| INDEX KEY ** | 56 - 57 |
| NUMBERS AND COUNTING * | 57 - 61 |
| GENERAL VOCABULARY * | 61 - 64 |
| CLOTHING, TRAINING AND LESSONS * | 64 - 68 |
| FORMS * | 68 - 71 |
| SPARRING * | 71 - 73 |
| COMPETITIONS, EXAMINATIONS AND EVENTS * | 73 - 75 |
| EQUIPMENT * | 75 - 76 |
| VIRTUES AND MORALITY * | 76 - 78 |
| NOMINALISED VERBS ** | 78 - 80 |
| BODY PARTS AND CRITICAL POINTS * | 80 - 84 |
| STRIKING SURFACES AND HAND FORMATIONS * | 85 - 88 |
| DIRECTIONS * | 88 - 91 |
| STANCES AND SHIFTING * | 91 - 95 |
| BLOCKING * | 95 - 98 |
| KICKING * | 98 - 101 |
| PUNCHING * | 101 - 103 |
| STRIKING * | 103 - 105 |
| THRUSTING * | 105 - 107 |
| GRASPING AND RELEASING * | 107 - 108 |
| OTHER TECHNIQUES * | 108 |

| | |
|---|---|
| WEAPONS ** | 109 |
| TITLES AND HONORIFICS *** | 109 - 112 |
| SALUTATIONS *** | 112 - 113 |
| COMMANDS * | 113 - 115 |
| RELATED VOCABULARY *** | 116 - 117 |
| FORMING MOVEMENT NAMES *** | 117 - 118 |
| ⑤ **CONVERSATION** | **119 - 122** |
| IN LESSONS *** | 120 |
| OUT OF LESSONS *** | 120 - 121 |
| ⑥ **CONCLUSION** | **123 - 139** |
| EXAMPLES OF MISTAKES * | 124 - 125 |
| ABOUT THE AUTHOR | 125 - 127 |
| WRITING THE BOOK | 127 - 128 |
| COPYRIGHT | 128 - 129 |
| REMINDER NOTICE | 128 - 129 |
| SPECIAL NOTICE | 129 |
| AUDIO CD TRACKS | 130 - 133 |
| BLANK NOTES PAGES | |

㉠

기원와역사

② Origins and History

# Overview

Korean is the fourteenth most spoken language in the world, now with approximately seventy-eight million speakers of it across the world. In the history of Korea, there have been two different languages under the category of Korean. In this book, both are used on occasion, although the latter of the following far more often.

Like many Asian languages, Korea shares elements with the Chinese languages, which have their influence across East Asia. In its modern form, there are still many words which remain the same.

# Hanja

Hanja is an older, evolved language from Chinese that was spoken up until the late nineteenth and twentieth century. Due to the location and terrain of the Korean peninsula, where it was easier to get to the mainland by crossing the ocean, the sounds of the language transformed with Mandarin and Cantonese influences from along what is now the coastline of China.

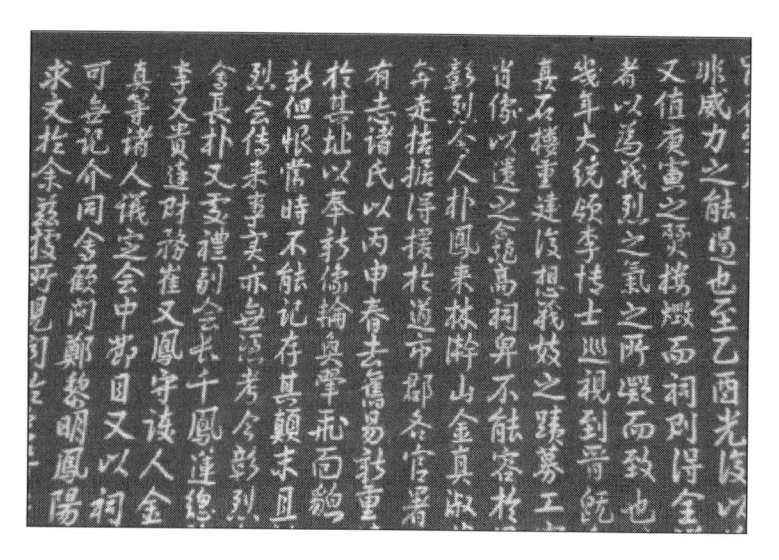

*Above: old Hanja text on a wall in Jinju Castle in Gyeongsangnamdo Province.*

The written form of the language conversely, remained the same. All the symbols match those of Traditional Chinese, and for people who cannot read them, will look identical. Accordingly, like the languages which it comes from, Hanja is not grounded on any phonetic system. Each specific character has a selection of syllables that it can be, but there is no relation between the components of the character and its pronunciation.

For a long time it was necessary to be fluent in reading and writing Hanja in order to be literate in Korean, as the vast majority of Korean literature and most other Korean documents were written in Hanja. But due to the complexity of the symbols, being literate was only attainable by the aristocracy. This ultimately meant that the average person in Korea was illiterate, whilst this language was in use.

Nowadays Hanja cannot be used to write native Korean words, those which have been invented since the instigation of the new language, such words are always rendered in Hangeul. Words of Chinese origin are written with the Hangeul alphabet almost all the time. Hanja is rarely seen in modern Korea.

Hanja now plays a different role. Scholars who seek to study Korean history must unsurprisingly study Hanja in order to read original historical manuscripts. It has also been popularised as a formal, ceremonial, and decorative language recently, as many people find it to be a more beautiful and impressive writing system. It is gradually being revived in South Korea through people's personal interest.

In Taekwondo Hanja is sometimes used for similar reasons and because there are often occurrences where it is pertinent. You might occasionally see it on certificates at higher levels or older documents. It would also be pleasant to see it at official events.

This book provides some Hanja for such instances. It is extremely complicated, and unless you have had an introduction to Chinese, I would not recommend trying to reproduce it by hand. I have added the Hanja for some appropriate words, where I think that the word could be used in a more formal context such as exams or competitions. But for most of the movement words, the core of the terminology, there is no Hanja because these are new, native words.

# Hangeul

The language of Hanja, as mentioned, is now no longer the dominant dialect of Korea. The common script now is Hangeul, which uses all the same syllables as Hanja, but uses a much easier phonetic system. This breaks down the previous pictorial symbols into their component sounds, and rewrites them using much simpler lettering. Hence Hangeul can not only enable straightforward representation of the current Hanja words, but even be used to create new ones.

This gives Koreans several advantages when it comes to foreign languages, the vast majority of which can be reconstructed roughly in their own language. This is the case with many internationally used English words, which can be written in Hangeul with limited accuracy.

Hangeul is regarded as an atypical language by professionals because it is one of the few to have been invented, rather than to have initially evolved. Hangeul was promulgated by the fourth king of the Joseon Dynasty, Sejong the Great, whose statue is on the cover of this book.

In explaining the necessity for the new script, King Sejong believed that the Korean language was different from Chinese; using Hanja to write was so difficult for the common people that only the privileged could read and write fluently. The majority of Koreans were effectively uneducated before the invention of Hangeul.

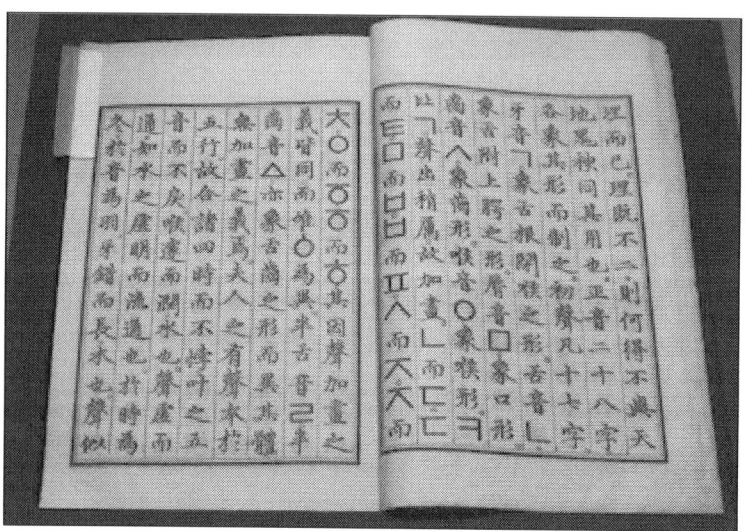

*Above: Hunminjeong-eum Haerye.*

The people could speak the language, but not relate it to words on a page. King Sejong set to work with his scholars to devise a structure whereby the pronunciation of a character would relate to its component parts, so as to provide a writing system for the current language. The project was completed in late December 1443 or January 1444, and described in 1446 in a document titled *Hunminjeong-eum - the Proper Sounds for the Education of the People*, after which the alphabet itself was named.

The language was constructed with the intention that the average person could effortlessly learn to read and write, with the famous quote: *"A wise man could acquaint himself with them before the morning is over; a stupid man can learn them in the space of ten days."* from the book *Hunminjeongeum Haerye*, a commentary of the original script.

*Above: modern Hangeul on an airport sign at Incheon International Airport.*

Hangeul faced opposition by the literate elite, who believed Hanja to be the only legitimate writing system, and perhaps saw it as a threat to their status. Nevertheless, it entered popular culture as the king had intended, being used especially by women and writers of popular fiction.

Since gaining independence from Japan, the Koreas have used Hangeul or mixed Hangeul as their sole official writing system, with ever-decreasing use of Hanja. Since the 1950s, it has become uncommon to find Hanja in commercial or unofficial writing in the South. North Korea instated Hangeul as its exclusive writing system in 1949, and banned the use of Hanja completely.

But the language is not only special due to the fact that it was invented, but it unintentionally combines elements that are common to eastern and western languages to make a notably unique language. The western languages, those which emanated from Europe, have the common feature that they are phonetically based, albeit a very loose phonetic system. The eastern languages are typically written in blocks of equal size according to syllable. Hangeul is one of the few languages to actually combine these two elements.

By the end of this book, depending on how far you choose to take learning Korean, you will hopefully be able to identify between Korean and other oriental languages, a skill lost on most people.

㊂

# 언어의 기술와 개념

③

# Language Skills and Concepts

# Sounds and Pronunciation

## Vowels

In English, we have more vowel sounds than we do vowel characters. As you learn Korean you will start to notice this. In our language, one can radically adjust the sound of a vowel and hence the sound of a word, yet still be perfectly understood. For example, how many different ways can you think of pronouncing each vowel letter? This manifests itself predominantly through accents, which are widely mutually intelligible.

In Korean there is also a slight disparity in the pronunciation and intonation of vowels, but it is not as prominent as the vowel sounds are more precise. Thus there are accents in Korean, though they are narrower than in English, and morphed sounds cannot be so readily understood.

Depending on how one considers the sounds phonologically, one could declare more or fewer vowels in Korean, but for simplicity, there are eight main sounds.

| Character | Sound |
|---|---|
| ㅏ | "*a*" as in "*father*", "*laugh*" or "*grass*" |
| ㅓ | "*eo*" is a sound somewhere between "*on*" and "*but*" |
| ㅗ | "*o*" as in "*order*", "*claw*", or "*thought*" |
| ㅜ | "*u*" as in "*food*", "*choose*" or "*hoover*" |
| ㅡ | "*eu*" as in "*look*", "*put*" or "*should*" |
| ㅣ | "*i*" as in "*even*", "*meet*" or "*leak*" |
| ㅔ | "*e*" as in "*pen*" or "*then*" |

| | | |
|---|---|---|
| ㅐ | "*ae*" is roughly between the sounds of "*<u>ai</u>r*" and "*b<u>a</u>t*" | + |

You will notice that there are two characters at the end of this list, marked with the + symbol, which actually are each two of the previous characters written together. The penultimate vowel is a combination of the "*eo*" and "*i*" characters; the final vowel is a combination of the "*a*" and "*i*" characters. These represent a mergence of the sounds that each character represents alone. However for the purposes of this course it is best just to consider these two vowels to be unique characters.

From these basic sounds we can do two things in Korean. At the beginning of some of the sounds we can either add a "*y*" sound or a "*w*" sound. Not all of the characters however, can have this, for the obvious reason that "*y*" is essentially a short "*i*" sound and "*w*" a short "*u*" sound. You cannot put the one sound before the same sound, as it would make no difference to the vowel, so we cannot write "*yi*" or "*wu*", along with some others.

Some vowel characters have a dash coming off the main line. It is these characters which we can add the "*y*" sound to easily by placing a second dash off of the character. This adds the "*y*" sound to the beginning of the vowel. There are two characters which have no dash and are just straight lines, these characters cannot have the "*y*" sound added.

| Character | Sound |
|---|---|
| ㅑ | "*ya*" like "*<u>ya</u>rd*" |
| ㅕ | "*yeo*" like "*<u>ya</u>cht*" or "*<u>yo</u>ghurt*" |
| ㅛ | "*yo*" as in "*<u>yo</u>ur*" or "*<u>ya</u>wn*" |
| ㅠ | "*yu*" sounding like "*<u>you</u>*" or "*<u>u</u>sual*" |
| ㅖ | "*ye*" like "*<u>ye</u>s*" or "*<u>ye</u>sterday*" |
| ㅒ | "*yae*" is pronounced similarly to "*ye*" above as in "*<u>ye</u>llow*" |

Making the *"w"* sound is not so simple. For this you must add either the *"u"*, *"o"* or *"eu"* sounds beforehand, giving the same affect as *"w"*.

| Character | Sound |
|---|---|
| 과 | *"wa"* as in *"qu<u>a</u>ck"* |
| 궈 | *"wo"* like *"<u>wo</u>nder"*, *"<u>wha</u>t"* or *"<u>o</u>ne"* |
| 괘 | *"wae"* like *"<u>whe</u>re"* |
| 궤 | *"we"* like *"<u>wa</u>ve"* or *"<u>way</u>"* |
| 괴 | *"oi"* is pronounced similarly to *"wae"* above but more like *"t<u>oy</u>"* |
| 의 | *"ui"* sounding similar to *"<u>wei</u>rd"* |
| 귀 | *"wi"* just like *"<u>we</u>"* |

Korean is capable of expressing hundreds more obsolete vowel sounds, although these are not used in the most common words, and there are none in the words listed in the main index of this book. The vowel characters here are all those that can be written using a standard Korean keyboard, and hence are in the most common use.

# Consonants

An important point to start with is that there is a complete absence of *"f"* and *"v"* sounds in Korean, which is peculiar as the language from which it is ultimately derived, Chinese, does have the sound *"f"*. In historical documents relating to the creation of the language, there appear to be some characters that might potentially have been these sounds, but for some reason they never survived into the modern language.

Korean also does not use the *"th"* sound, although this is not surprising as it is rare among languages. With whatever list of terminology you currently use you may or may not have noticed this. Hence if you see a list of terminology claiming to have a word with any of these impossible sounds in it, you know instantly that it is incorrect.

There are otherwise fourteen main consonant sounds in Korean, and five very common double consonant sounds. Whilst we will come across some less frequently seen double consonants, the majority of the language uses these next nineteen sounds.

The consonants have been split into two tables. You will notice that the consonants in the first table have similarities, according to which they can be sorted into groups of three. The same basic character, with slight differences, is used to represent the same basic sounds, with slight differences.

In each group there is a heavily aspirated, slightly aspirated, and an unaspirated consonant. Aspiration refers to the amount of breath released with the consonant. For example, in English, we have the basic sounds *"j"* and *"ch"*. When you say *"ch"* you release move of a breath than when you say *"j"*, hence *"ch"* is more heavily aspirated.

| Character | Sound |
|---|---|
| ㄲ | unaspirated; sounds like a heavy *"g"* as in *"good"* or *"green"* |
| ㄱ | lightly aspirated; in between the above and below sounds |
| ㅋ | heavily aspirated; such as *"call"* or *"keen"* |
| ㄸ | unaspirated; *"d"* like *"dog"* or *"debt"* |
| ㄷ | lightly aspirated; in between the above and below sounds |
| ㅌ | heavily aspirated; *"t"* like *"tick"* or *"tall"* |
| ㅉ | unaspirated; *"j"* like *"jog"* or *"drive"* |
| ㅈ | lightly aspirated; in between the above and below sounds |
| ㅊ | heavily aspirated; *"ch"* like *"cheap"* or *"chicken"* |
| ㅃ | unaspirated; *"b"* as in *"bad"* or *"bottle"* |

| Character | Sound |
|---|---|
| ㅂ | lightly aspirated; in between the above and below sounds |
| ㅍ | heavily aspirated; "p" as in "<u>p</u>ink" or "<u>p</u>ineapple" |

Whilst the double consonants here could be considered like all others, in that they are merely an amalgamation of sounds; the combination they provide is quite elementary to the language. These particular double consonants are used very often throughout the language.

The second group of consonants does not follow the idea of varying degrees of aspiration. These consonants are often found to be much easier to say by Westerners.

| Character | Sound |
|---|---|
| ㅁ | "m" as in "<u>m</u>ouse" |
| ㄴ | "n" like "<u>n</u>ecklace" or "<u>n</u>ew" |
| ㅇ | "ng" as in "ki<u>ng</u>" or "thi<u>ng</u>", and is also used as a silent consonant |
| ㄹ | "l" as in "<u>l</u>eak" or "r" as in "<u>r</u>ed" |
| ㅎ | "h" sounding like "<u>h</u>at" |
| ㅅ | a gentle "s" sound like "<u>s</u>ong" |
| ㅆ | a tense "s" sound, similar but not the same as "z" |

You will have noticed that there is another double consonant at the end here. This works in just the same way as the other double consonants. It intensifies the sound, and one enunciates it with a much tenser jaw.

It is often said how many Koreans cannot distinguish between the "r" and the "l" sound when they speak English. This is not surprising, because the sounds are represented by the same character in Korean. The character is nearly always pronounced as an "l", except where there are vowels either side of it within the word, where it is pronounced like "r".

It is important to note, that the Korean consonants, unlike the vowels, sometimes change according to their position within the word. This is partly due to the original rules, and partly due to colloquial adjustments. We will look at which consonants change and how in the next section.

# Characters

## Components

Just as there are particular ways to inscribe the English characters, there are also specific sequences and patterns that you should follow when writing Korean symbols. In oriental languages this is called a stroke order, where you are supposed to draw each of the component lines in a precise order and direction, in order to get the correct proportion and shape to the character. The stroke order rules are the following.

- Write each component character separately.
- Start with the strokes at the top and move down.
- If many strokes are at the same level, start with the strokes to the left and move right.
- Write horizontal strokes from left to right.
- Write vertical strokes from top to bottom.
- Write falling strokes from top to bottom.
- Write left falling strokes before right falling ones.
- Draw circular strokes anticlockwise.

These rules are mimicked through the following diagrams, which you can use alternatively to memorising the rules. The first table describes only the simple vowels. The more complex vowels follow the same ideas.

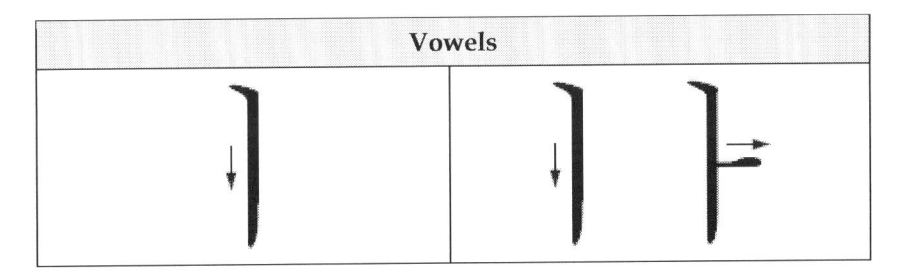

| Vowels |
| --- |
| ㅣ      ㅣ ㅏ |

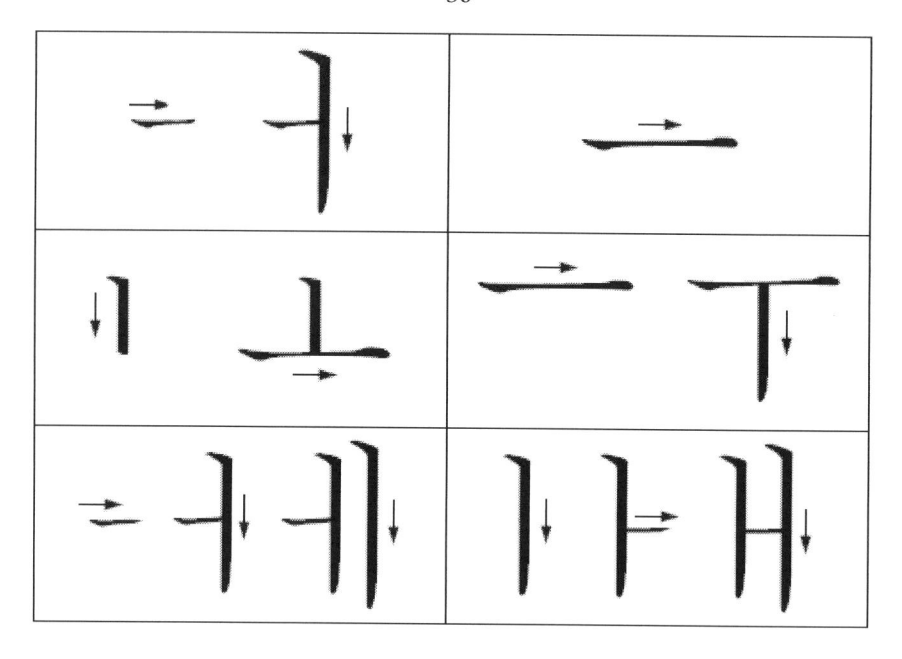

This following table excludes the main double consonants. To write these, simply write the two consonants next to each other, whether they are the same consonant or two different ones.

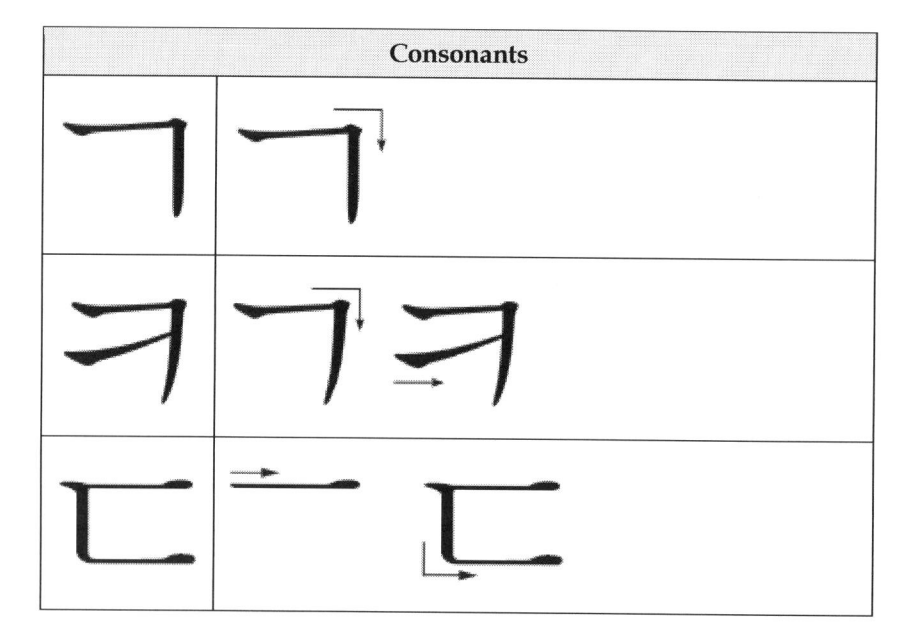

| Consonants ||
|---|---|
| ㄱ | ㄱ |
| ㅋ | ㅋ ㅋ |
| ㄷ | ㄷ ㄷ |

| ㅌ | ㅡ ㅡ ㅌ |
| ㅈ | ㅡ ㄱ ㅈ |
| ㅊ | ㅡ ㅡ ㅜ ㅊ |
| ㅂ | ㅣ ㅣ ㅐ ㅂ |
| ㅍ | ㅡ ㄱ ㅠ ㅍ |
| ㅁ | ㅣ ㄱ ㅁ |
| ㄴ | ㄴ |
| ㅇ | ㅇ |

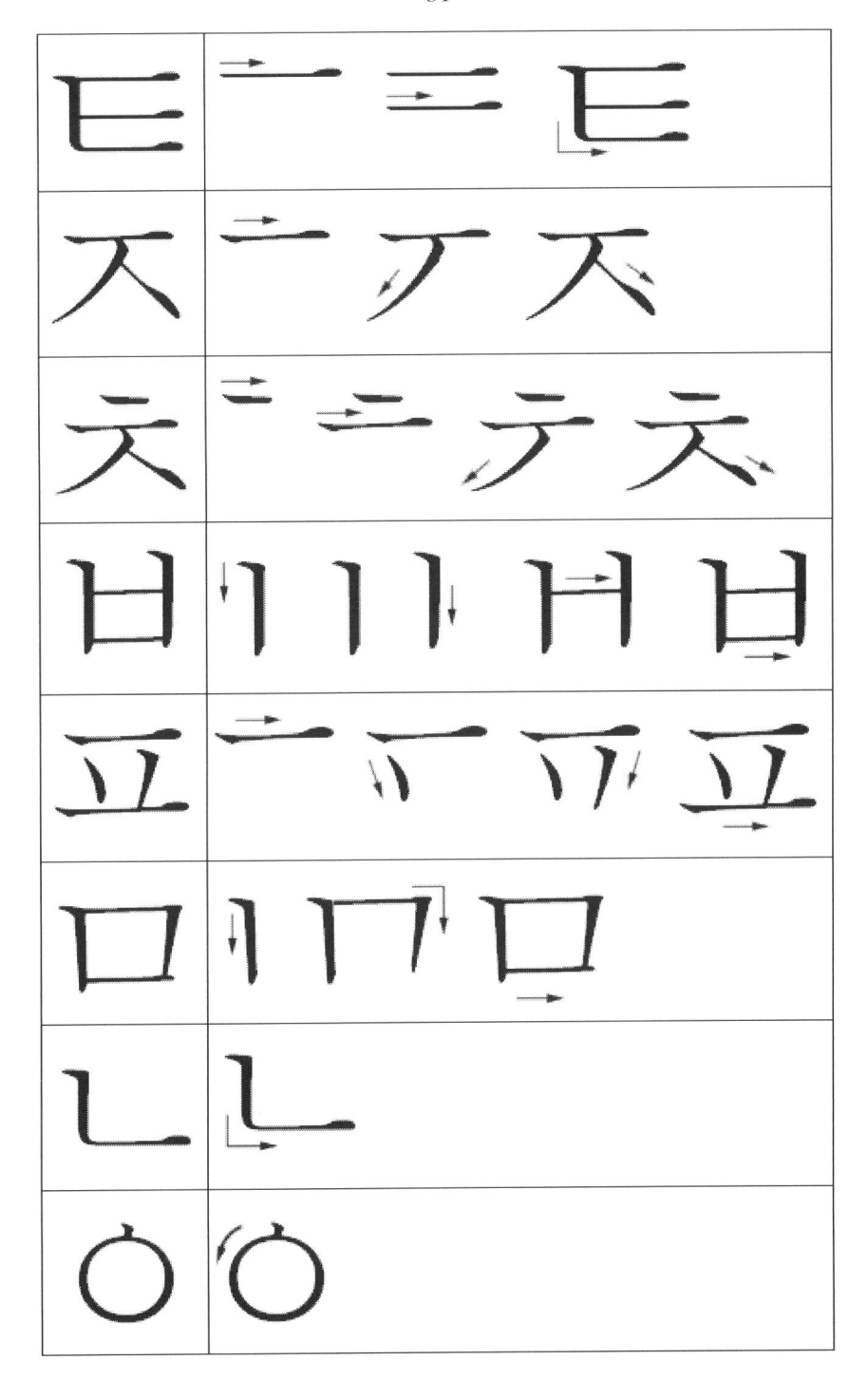

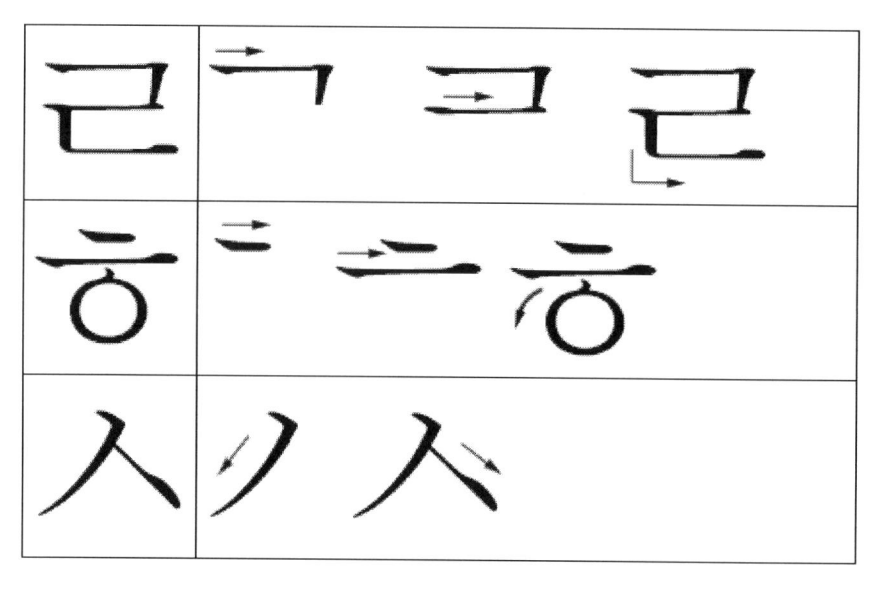

In western languages we give our letters names. These are often short syllables that contain the sound of their associated character, and in many cases the names are so basic that we don't think of them as words. This is roughly similar to Korean, where each consonant does have a specific name. This is obviously useful for discussion of the characters. The following table uses the romanisation systems that are explained later.

| Character | Name | | |
|---|---|---|---|
| ㄲ | 쌍기역 | ssanggiyeok | SK |
|    | 쌍기윽 | ssanggieuk | NK |
| ㄱ | 기역 | giyeok | SK |
|    | 기윽 | gieuk | NK |
| ㅋ | 키읔 | kieuk | |
| ㄸ | 쌍디귿 | ssangdigeut | SK |
|    | 쌍디읃 | ssangdieut | NK |

| ㄷ | 디귿 | digeut | SK |
|---|---|---|---|
|  | 디읃 | dieut | NK |
| ㅌ | 티읕 | tieut |  |
| ㅉ | 쌍지읒 | ssangjieut |  |
| ㅈ | 지읒 | jieut |  |
| ㅊ | 치읓 | chieut |  |
| ㅃ | 쌍비읍 | ssangbieup |  |
| ㅂ | 비읍 | bieup |  |
| ㅍ | 피읖 | pieup |  |
| ㅁ | 미음 | mieum |  |
| ㄴ | 니은 | nieun |  |
| ㅇ | 이응 | ieung |  |
| ㄹ | 리을 | rieul |  |
| ㅎ | 히읗 | hieut |  |
| ㅅ | 시옷 | shiot | SK |
|  | 시읏 | shieut | NK |

| ㅆ | 쌍시옷 | ssangshiot | SK |
|---|---|---|---|
|   | 쌍시읏 | ssangshieut | NK |

The vowels conversely are just named by the sound that they represent.

## Syllables

Syllables in Korean must comprise of at least two elements: an initial, and a medial. The initial is always a consonant and the medial is always a vowel. You can however, have the silent consonant as the initial, leaving just the sound of the vowel.

You can also incorporate an optional third element: a final. The final must also be a consonant. You can choose any consonant or any vowel for the appropriate position, to make a syllable.

Whilst in English we write our letters in a continuous line, in Korean the characters are arranged into blocks which represent each syllable. Depending on which component characters need to be written, a different design of syllable block is used. The rules to decide this are quite simple. The arrangement of the block depends on the vowel, as some are horizontal, some are vertical, and in some cases both.

To demonstrate this, we will start by looking at examples of syllables containing just two elements: the initial and the medial. Here are some syllables which have medials with a vertical axis. The initial consonant is written on the left, and the medial vowel is written on the right when the medial contains a vertical axis.

가 지 너 매 베

|  Initial  |  Medial  |

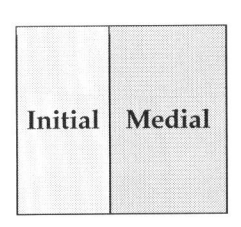

Here are some syllables which have medials with a horizontal axis. The initial is written at the top, and the medial is written underneath if the vowel is predominantly horizontal.

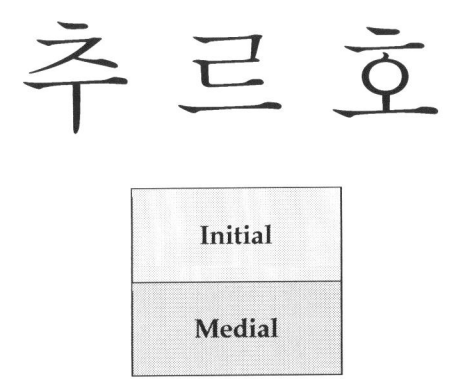

추 르 호

| Initial |
| Medial |

In some cases, the vowel contains both a horizontal and vertical element. In this case we apply both techniques together to get to following shapes.

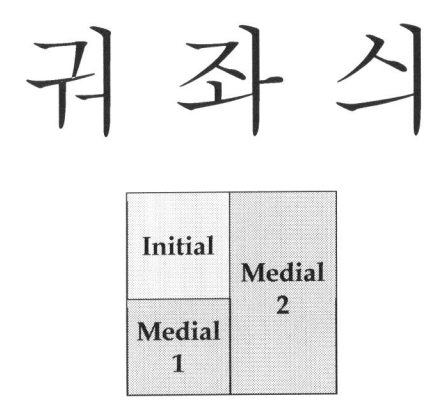

궈 좌 싀

| Initial | Medial 2 |
| Medial 1 | |

This forms the basis of all syllabic blocks. If we were to add a final sound, the character is merely added underneath the remainder of the syllable.

# 당 줄 권

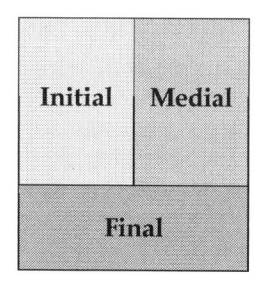

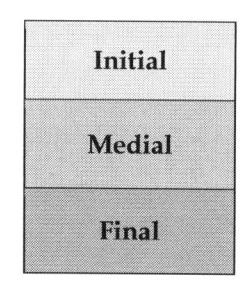

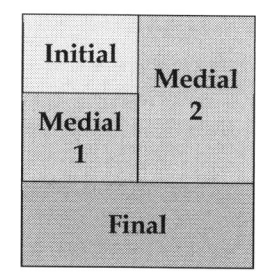

|                          |                  |                          |
|--------------------------|------------------|--------------------------|
| Initial \| Medial        | Initial          | Initial \| Medial 2      |
|                          | Medial           | Medial 1 \|              |
| Final                    | Final            | Final                    |

Remember that a consonant sound, so an initial or a final, can consist of two component characters: a double consonant. A double consonant can be two different component characters, or the same one; some are more common than others. In this situation, the two components of the consonant are written side by side in whichever part of the syllabic block they go. Here are some examples of this.

# 뛰 빽 넗 줒 꼠

Syllabic blocks should always remain a constant size, and so when writing them, you need to alter the proportions of the component characters to fit. As you can see, when there are many components, everything must squash together.

Whenever you write syllabic blocks, you should write them in the order of their sound: initial, medial, final.

If we want to create just a vowel sound with no consonant sound before it, then we use the silent consonant in the initial position.

# 아 인 오 을 웅

If however, we use the same character in the final position, it changes to its *"ng"* sound. This is an example of how the sounds of some component characters change according to their position within the syllable. Most of the consonants will stay the same whether they are in the initial or the final position. Including the one we just looked at, there are four main changes.

| Character | Initial Sound | Final Sound |
|---|---|---|
| ㅇ | silent | *"ng"* as in *"king"* or *"thing"* |
| ㅈ ㅉ ㅊ | *"j"* or *"ch"* | *"t"* |
| ㅅ ㅆ | *"s"* | *"t"* |
| ㅎ | *"h"* | *"t"* |
| ㄹ | *"r"* | *"l"* |

These changes are important as you will see them frequently in the terminology listed in this book. It is important to know that these changes always occur unless the following syllable in the same word starts with a vowel, when they return to their initial sound.

There are many more consonant transformations which involve more complicated consonants, many of them double consonants. These are covered later in the romanisation tables.

# Alphabetical Order

The alphabetical order of all the Korean characters has been revised many times in history. Whilst the language was initially devised, it has still evolved since its foundation, simultaneously bringing about amendments to the characters included in the official alphabet, resulting in its reconstruction.

Originally the alphabet incorporated just the basic characters; nowadays however, it lists many of the common compound characters, though leaving out the obsolete ones.

North Korea maintains quite a traditional order, placing new letters towards the end of each series.

| North Korean Order |
|---|
| **Initials** |
| ㄱ ㄴ ㄷ ㄹ ㅁ ㅂ ㅅ ㅈ ㅊ ㅋ ㅌ ㅍ ㅎ ㄲ ㄸ ㅃ ㅆ ㅉ ㅇ |
| **Medials** |
| ㅏ ㅑ ㅓ ㅕ ㅗ ㅛ ㅜ ㅠ ㅡ ㅣ ㅐ ㅒ ㅔ ㅖ ㅚ ㅟ ㅢ ㅘ ㅝ ㅙ ㅞ |
| **Finals** |
| ㄱ ㄳ ㄴ ㄵ ㄶ ㄷ ㄹ ㄺ ㄻ ㄼ ㄽ ㄾ ㄿ ㅀ ㅁ ㅂ ㅄ ㅅ ㅇ ㅈ ㅊ ㅋ ㅌ ㅍ ㅎ ㄲ ㅆ |

South Korea has adjusted the order to present perhaps a more logical sequence.

| South Korean Order |
|---|
| **Initials** |
| ㄱ ㄲ ㄴ ㄷ ㄸ ㄹ ㅁ ㅂ ㅃ |

| ㅅ ㅆ ㅇ ㅈ ㅉ ㅊ ㅋ ㅌ ㅍ |
| ㅎ |

**Medials**

| ㅏ ㅐ ㅑ ㅒ ㅓ ㅔ ㅕ ㅖ ㅗ |
| ㅘ ㅙ ㅚ ㅛ ㅜ ㅝ ㅞ ㅟ ㅠ |
| ㅡ ㅢ ㅣ |

**Finals**

| ㄱ ㄲ ㄳ ㄴ ㄵ ㄶ ㄷ ㄹ ㄺ |
| ㄻ ㄼ ㄽ ㄾ ㄿ ㅀ ㅁ ㅂ ㅄ |
| ㅅ ㅆ ㅇ ㅈ ㅊ ㅋ ㅌ ㅍ ㅎ |

# Romanisation

In order to make learning Korean easier, and so that non speakers can pronounce Korean words without learning the language, there needs to be a system of representing the Korean characters with Latin letters. There are three main systems for representing the Korean characters with English or letters or deviations thereupon: McCune-Reischauer, Yale, and Revised.

## McCune-Reischauer and Yale Systems

These are the two standard systems for writing Korean using roman based lettering.

McCune–Reischauer romanisation is one of the two most widely used Korean language romanisation systems. It was created in 1937 by two

Americans: George M. McCune and Edwin O. Reischauer. With a few exceptions, it does not attempt to transliterate Hangeul but rather to represent the phonetic pronunciation. The system uses almost all English letters, apart from two: ŭ and ŏ. These extra two are used because of the additional vowels in Korean, but look familiar to the English speaker by the use of the breves.

The system is regarded highly and has been used predominantly of all the systems; however it has some major downfalls. It is largely unpredictable, you need to use reference tables a lot in order to Romanise according to this system, and once Romanised, whilst it is then easier to read, it is incredibly difficult to change it back into Hangeul.

It also requires a lot of additional punctuation and marks, which are vital to the system, in order to convey the sounds properly. Certainly if you are using a computer, this can take a very long time.

The Yale system, developed by Samuel Elmo Martin and his colleagues at Yale University about half a decade after McCune-Reischauer, has the specific purpose of being used for technical language skills. It has sibling systems for other oriental languages developed in a similar manner. It is still used today, although mainly by linguists, among whom it has become the standard romanisation for the language. If you were studying a specific attribute to the Korean language, even writing a thesis on it, you would certainly use Yale.

The Yale system places primary emphasis on showing a word's morphophonemic structure. This distinguishes it from the other two widely used systems for romanising Korean. These two usually provide the pronunciation for an entire word, but the morphophonemic elements accounting for that pronunciation often can not be recovered from the romanisations, which makes them ill-suited for linguistic use.

It is not practical however, to be used by the everyday westerner trying to pronounce Korean words. It includes many more extra characters, and other characters are incredibly misleading to beginners, such as the "*j*" sound is represented with the letter *c*. It also does not add in helpful Romanisation rules, for example, the letter *l* is never changed to *r* when pronounced as "*r*", nor does *s* change to *sh* when pronounced so. For someone who has never read the rules, pronunciation would be completely impossible.

# Revised System

The Revised Romanisation System of Korean was introduced at the start of the millennium. It is based largely on the McCune-Reischauer system but with a few modifications to suit its purpose. The revised system has three key aims: firstly to be written on computer, particularly the internet. It is not possible to write the extra two vowels in domain names. Secondly, people would often not bother writing all the extra punctuation or inflections required by the McCune-Reischauer system; hence it would technically change the sound of the word. This is one of the contributing problems as to why we have such incorrect terminology in Taekwondo. Thirdly, the McCune-Reischauer system looks so alien to most westerners that they can't pronounce it. For those who have English as a second language, additional markings make it impossible to read. By modelling the new system on English the Korean government made it possible for many more people to read it.

The revised system is good, and definitely achieves its aims. In this book, the system we will use is almost identical to it, but with a few further modifications. Here are the Romanisation tables for the revised system. You don't need to learn these at all, but this just provides proof that we have derived the vocabulary from the Korean itself.

| ㅏ | ㅓ | ㅗ | ㅜ | ㅡ | ㅣ | ㅐ |
|---|---|---|---|---|---|---|
| *a* | *eo* | *o* | *u* | *eu* | *i* | *ae* |
| ㅔ | ㅑ | ㅕ | ㅛ | ㅠ | ㅒ | ㅖ |
| *e* | *ya* | *yeo* | *yo* | *yu* | *yae* | *ye* |
| ㅘ | ㅙ | ㅝ | ㅞ | ㅢ | ㅚ | ㅟ |
| *wa* | *wae* | *wo* | *we* | *ui* | *oe* | *wi* |

| ㄱ | ㄲ | ㅋ | ㄷ | ㄸ | ㅌ | ㅂ |
|---|---|---|---|---|---|---|
| *g, k* | *kk* | *k* | *d, t* | *tt* | *t* | *b, p* |

| ㅃ | ㅍ | ㅈ | ㅉ | ㅊ | ㅅ | ㅆ |
|----|----|----|----|----|----|----|
| pp | p  | j  | jj | ch | s  | ss |
| ㅎ | ㄴ | ㅁ | ㅇ | ㄹ |    |    |
| h  | n  | m  | ng | r, l |  |    |

In Korean, there are certain phonetic changes that occur depending on the final consonant of the syllable before, which are sometimes surprising. To avoid having to remember these, they are included into the romanisation system. This table lists all the finals and initials and how they change when put together, bearing in mind that many of them do not.

| Final \ Initial | | ㅇ | ㄱ | ㄴ | ㄷ | ㄹ | ㅁ | ㅂ |
|---|---|---|---|---|---|---|---|---|
|   |   | - | g | n | d | r | m | b |
| ㄱ | k | g | kg | ngn | kd | ngn | ngm | kb |
| ㄴ | n | n | n-g | nn | nd | ll, nn | nm | nb |
| ㄷ | t | d, j | tg | nn | td | nn | nm | tb |
| ㄹ | l | r | lg | ll, nn | ld | ll | lm | lb |
| ㅁ | m | m | mg | mn | md | mn | mm | mb |
| ㅂ | p | b | pg | mn | pd | mn | mm | pb |
| ㅇ | ng | ng- | ngg | ngn | ngd | ngn | ngm | ngb |

| Final \ Initial | ㅅ s | ㅈ j | ㅊ ch | ㅋ k | ㅌ t | ㅍ p | ㅎ h |
|---|---|---|---|---|---|---|---|
| ㄱ k | ks | kj | kch | k-k | kt | kp | kh, k |
| ㄴ n | ns | nj | nch | nk | nt | np | nh |
| ㄷ t | ts | tj | tch | tk | t-t | tp | th, t, ch |
| ㄹ l | ls | lj | lch | lk | lt | lp | lh |
| ㅁ m | ms | mj | mch | mk | mt | mp | mh |
| ㅂ p | ps | pj | pch | pk | pt | p-p | ph, p |
| ㅇ ng | ngs | ngj | ngch | ngk | ngt | ngp | ngh |

| ㄱㅅ | ㅂㅅ | ㄹㅅ | ㄹㅌ | ㄹㅐ | ㄴㅈ |
|---|---|---|---|---|---|
| k | p | l | l | l | n |
| ㄹㅎ | ㄴㅎ | ㄹㄱ | ㄹㅁ | ㄹㅍ | |
| l | n | k | m | p | |

These romanisation tables show you how to change the Hangeul script into the characters of the English alphabet.

## Our System

Next we have a list of modifications. Generally these are just statements that we will be taking many of the optional Romanisation techniques. These determine how we will do things differently in this book.

- In the original system, writing *sh* where it is pronounced so is optional, however in this book it is always written *sh* where it is pronounced "*sh*".
- If a "*j*" or "*s*" final sound is pronounced "*t*", then it is written as t.
- Interchanging between *l* and *r* is always made to suit the pronounced sound without exception. This again, is optional in the revised system.
- There are some words, such as *Taekwondo* or *Choi Hong Hi*, which have been romanised in other systems and we are used to seeing in that very specific way, despite the fact that the revised system would have them written differently. Such traditional words are not altered in their "English" name; however the romanisation is still done according to the new system.
- Sometimes the same symbols are romanised slightly differently, either to reflect a change in pronunciation or to better convey the correct pronunciation. For example: sometimes *oe* is written as *oi*, as in *Choi Hong Hi*, but can also be written as *oe* as in *oebal seogi*. This is done to reduce confusion and get better pronunciation.

Here are the supplementary romanisation tables based on these modifications

| 시 | 슈 | 샤 | 셔 | 쇼 |
|---|---|---|---|---|
| *shi* | *shyu* | *shya* | *shyeo* | *shyo* |
| 씨 | 쓔 | 쌰 | 쎠 | 쑈 |
| *sshi* | *sshyu* | *sshya* | *sshyeo* | *sshyo* |

| 귀 | ㅢ | ㅚ |
|---|---|---|
| *wi* | *ui* | *oi, oe* |

These tables have been added to the book so that should you want, you can see how each of the words listed in the vocabulary section is derived, rather than just believe what is written. This solves one of the problems with most terminology lists; there is no evidence.

From now on all Korean will be romanised according to this system.

# Simple Grammar

## Sentence Structure

The fundamental construction of the Korean language is different from English. In English, our grammatical structure follows the order: subject, verb, and then object. The verb is the action itself. The subject is that which enacts the verb, and undergoes the process of doing it. The object is what the verb is dealing with.

|  |  |  |
|---|---|---|
| | *I punch the target.* | |
| | *He shouts the command.* | |
| | *The Korean flag hangs on the wall.* | |
| Subject / Topic | Verb (Conjugated) | Object |
| *I* | *punch* | *the target* |
| *He* | *shouts* | *the command* |
| *The flag* | *hangs on* | *the wall* |

These are very simple sentences, but all sentences in English follow this basic pattern, although obviously you can make them far more complex.

In Korean, the grammatical structure follows a different order of: subject, object, and then verb. So the same sentence according to this pattern would be the following.

|  |  |  |
|---|---|---|
| | *I the target punch.* | |
| Subject / Topic | Object | Verb |
| *I* | *the target* | *punch* |

In these instances, the subject of the sentence, that which enacts the verb, is also the topic of the sentence, that which the sentence is about. You can have sentences where the topic and subject are separate.

| Speaking of this class, the students have good co-ordination. ||||
|---|---|---|---|
| Topic | Subject | Verb | Object |
| this class | the students | have | co-ordination |

## Case Particles

In order to specify which word is the subject, which is the topic, and which is the object, in Korean, you add a certain suffix onto the word to denote its purpose within the sentence. Adding suffixes is very common in Korean.

Each suffix has a different form, depending on whether the word ends with a vowel or a consonant.

|  | **Ends with Consonant** | **Ends with Vowel** |
|---|---|---|
| **Topic** | 이 | 가 |
|  | i | ga |
| **Subject** | 은 | 는 |
|  | eun | neun |
| **Object** | 을 | 를 |
|  | eul | reul |

In most instances, the subject and the topic of the sentence happen to be the same word. In this case one could either add the topic or the subject particle. By using the subject particle you are emphasising that word, whereas the topic particle is neutral.

| 차는 집 앞에 있어요 |
|---|
| cha<u>neun</u> jip ape isseoyo |
| <u>The car is</u> in front of the house. |

| |
|---|
| 차가 집 앞에 있어요 |
| *chaga jip ape isseoyo* |
| <u>There is a car</u> in front of the house. |

In these examples we might say it differently in English to change the importance of each of the ideas in the sentence.

# Verb Conjugation and Modification

The infinitive form of a verb is its root form, and that which is displayed in indexes or dictionaries. In English, we place the word *to* in front of the main verb word to make it into the infinitive, in Korean they add *da* to the end.

| <u>to</u> do | *ha<u>da</u>* | 하다 |
|---|---|---|
| <u>to</u> go | *ga<u>da</u>* | 가다 |
| <u>to</u> come | *o<u>da</u>* | 오다 |
| <u>to</u> be | *i<u>da</u>* | 이다 |
| <u>to</u> teach | *gareuchi<u>da</u>* | 가르치다 |
| <u>to</u> study | *gongbu ha<u>da</u>* | 공부하다 |

In English, the verb changes, conjugates, according to whom or what we are talking about. In Korean, the verb changes according to the relationship between the speaker and the listener. This is a vital aspect of Korean culture and language and an example of how honorifics are woven into it. Applying the speech level involves removing the infinitive ending and replacing it with an appropriate ending according to the level of formality that you intend.

# Formality and Respect

There are seven honorific levels in Korean to reflect the relationship between the people involved in the conversation and how much one honours it. Many of these are either rarely used, or have fallen into disuse, and in Taekwondo there are certainly only two which you will need to know. These are shaded in grey in the table, which lists all the speech levels.

| Name | Level of Formality | Usage |
|---|---|---|
| Hasoseoche 하소서체 | Extremely formal and polite | Traditionally used when addressing a king, queen, or high official; now used only in historical dramas. |
| Hapshyoche 합쇼체 | Formal and polite | Used commonly between strangers, among male co-workers, by TV announcers, and to customers. |
| Haoche 하오체 | Formal, of neutral politeness | Spoken form used nowadays only among some older people. Young people sometimes use it as an Internet dialect after it was popularised by historical dramas. |
| Hageche 하게체 | Formal, of neutral politeness | Generally used only by some older people when addressing younger people, friends, or relatives. |
| Haerache 해라체 | Formal, of neutral politeness or impolite | Used to close friends, relatives of similar age, or younger people; also used almost universally in books, newspapers, and magazines; also used in reported speech. |
| Haeyoche 해요체 | Informal and polite | Used mainly between strangers, especially those older or of equal age. Traditionally used more by women than men, though in Seoul many men prefer this form to the hapsyoche. |
| Haeche 해체 | Informal, of neutral politeness or impolite | Used most often between close friends and relatives, and when addressing younger people. Rarely used between strangers unless the speaker wishes to start a confrontation, or the listener is a child. |

The first, Hapshyoche, is formal and polite and should be used most of the time in Taekwondo, as you must have both of these attributes, regardless of the grade of the person you are speaking to. You would use this level of speech during lessons, or at competitions or gradings.

This speech level contains four types of verb ending, according to whether the sentence is a statement, question, command, or suggestion.

|  | Statement (Indicative) | Question (Interrogative) | Command (Imperative) | Suggestion (Hortative) |
|---|---|---|---|---|
| Verb stem ends with a vowel. | ㅂ니다<br>-mnida | ㅂ니까<br>-mnikka | ㅂ시요<br>-shipshiyo | ㅂ시다<br>-pshida |
| Verb stem ends with a consonant. | 읍니다<br>습니다<br>-eumnida<br>-seumnida | 읍니까<br>습니까<br>-eumnikka<br>-seumnikka | --십시요<br>-eushipshiyo | 읍시다<br>-eupshida |

To modify the verb into this speech level, one replaces the infinitive ending with the appropriate ending.

| |
|---|
| 저는 한국어를 공부합니다 |
| jeoneun hangugeoreul gongbuhamnida |
| I study Korean. |
| 선생은 무술을 가르칩니까 |
| seonsaeng-eun musureul gareuchimnikka |
| Do you teach martial arts? |
| 몸통 바치십시요 |
| momtong bachishipshiyo |
| Do press-ups! |
| 물 마십시다 |
| mul mashipshida |
| Let's drink some water. |

The second of the two speech levels, Haeyoche, you may need to use, is informal and polite, and you might use it before or after lessons when talking to other students, or if you meet them outside of any events. Though if the person you are talking to is a high ranking practitioner, you would always use the first one out of the two, never this speech level.

Unlike Hapshyoche, Haeyoche does not have different endings for different types of sentence; this is just implied in the same way it is in English, with tone and use of certain words.

| Infinitive ||| Modified ||
| English | Phonetic | Korean | Phonetic | Korean |
| --- | --- | --- | --- | --- |
| to do | hada | 하다 | haeyo | 해요 |
| to study | gongbu hada | 공부하다 | gongbu haeyo | 공부해요 |
| to exist | issda | 있다 | isseoyo | 있어요 |
| to learn | bae-uda | 배우다 | baewoyo | 배워요 |
| to teach | gareuchida | 가르치다 | gareuchieoyo | 가르치어요 |
| to read | ilkda | 익다 | ilgeoyo | 일거요 |
| to ask | mureoboda | 무러보다 | mureobwayo | 무러봐요 |
| to go | gada | 가다 | gayo | 가요 |
| to be so | geureohda | 그렇다 | geureohaeyo, geuraeyo | 그러해요 |
| to know | ada, alda | 아다, 알다 | areoyo | 아러요 |
| to meet | mannada | 만나다 | mannayo | 만나요 |
| to come | oda | 오다 | wayo | 와요 |
| to buy | sada | 사다 | sayo | 사요 |
| to like | johahada | 조하다 | johahaeyo | 조하해요 |
| to want | wonhada | 원하다 | wonhaeyo | 원해요 |
| to give | juda | 주다 | jueoyo | 주어요 |

There are several complicated patterns in how this speech level works, however these are unnecessary for the purposes of this book.

# Suffixes and Infixes

## Deductive Reasoning

Depending on the extensiveness of the terminology list you have been reading up until now, you may have noticed that there are some patterns to be established in the words. Here are some examples based on the list that I first used.

| Group 1 |
| --- |
| *sogi* |
| *jirugi* |
| *makgi* |
| *chagi* |
| *taerigi* |
| *tulgi* |

| Group 2 |
| --- |
| *naeryo* |
| *ollyo* |
| *hechyo* |
| *hullyo* |

A reminder that these words are not correctly romanised, don't use them to learn from.

You can see that in the first set, all the words end with the suffix *-gi*. They also commonly share the part of language that is nouns; they all describe the category of action you are performing. Therefore you can construe that there are a group of nouns ending in *-gi* in Korean. You also know that this rule can't be for all nouns, because for example, the noun *dobok* doesn't end in *-gi*, but perhaps there is another connection between those nouns which end with *-gi*.

In group two you can see that all words end with *-yo*. All these words are adjectives and adverbs, descriptive words. Again we can draw some conclusions from this. It is likely that because they all share a common attribute, that they are all formed in the same way from their root word.

# Regular Formation

Those two groups contain words which are not correctly romanised, and as such westerners pronounce the words differently. The suffixes that we have identified however are correct, so one can still find out much about the language even with a substandard list. One can find out much more though, if one has an accurate list.

If one were to glance across this list of terminology there are several endings that one would see often. These are: *-myeo, -ryeo, -lyeo, -yeo, -eo, -gi, -euro,* and *-ro*. Whilst these look like lots of different endings, they can be distilled into four groups according to the type of word one can identify it to be.

| Unusual Adjectives | Usual Adjectives | Nouns | Directions |
|---|---|---|---|
| *-myeo* | *-ryeo* | *-gi* | *-euro* |
|  | *-lyeo* |  | *-ro* |
|  | *-yeo* |  |  |
|  | *-eo* |  |  |

The last group here is a modification of a preposition. The two suffixes possess the same meaning, but if the preposition ends in a consonant, the suffix *-euro* is used, and if it ends in a vowel just *-ro* is used. If we have a preposition such as *wi* meaning *upper* or *above* and we modify it by placing *-ro* on the end to make *wiro* we change it to mean *upwards*. This suffixes gives the idea of going towards a position, so *apeuro* means forwards, *aneuro* means inwards and so on.

The first three groups here can replace the ending *-da* on a verb to make it a different type of word. Any word ending in with the first three groups of suffixes is a verb that has been changed into another type of word, such as a noun or adjective.

The usual adjectives actually all have the same ending, *-eo* which is changed to *-yeo* if the previous syllable ends in *i*, because *i* and *y* are essentially the same, and in Korean you can easily merge syllables in this way. The syllable then changes to *-ryeo* or *-lyeo* if the last syllable of the verb stem is *ri* or *li*. This happens to be a very common ending. If you want to make a verb into an adjective then you simply remove the ending *-da* and replace it with *-eo*, shortening it to *-yeo* if possible.

The *-myeo* ending does not work in the same way as those just mentioned; it has an independent meaning which gives it the idea of doing something as well. But the same method of forming the word applies for all of the first three groups.

| to Rise | *ollida* | 올리다 |
|---|---|---|

| a Rise | *olligi* | 올리기 |
|---|---|---|
| Rising | *ollyeo* | 올려 |
| whilst Rising | *ollimyeo* | 올리며 |

| to Strike, to Thrash | *ttaerida* | 때리다 |
|---|---|---|
| a Strike, a Thrash | *ttaerigi* | 때리기 |
| Striking | *ttaeryeo* | 때려 |
| whilst Striking | *ttaerimyeo* | 때리며 |

In the terminology section, only the most commonly used adjectives, adverbs and nouns are used, however if a word is in the above format, you know that you can derive other words from it should you need to.

# Irregular Formation

This technique for modifying verbs works most of the time, however as with all languages, every rule has an exception. There are some words which form irregular adjectives.

| to Block | *makda* | 막다 |
|---|---|---|
| a Block | *makgi* | 막기 |
| Blocking | *maga* | 막아 |

| to Grasp | *japda* | 잡다 |
|---|---|---|
| a Grasp | *japgi* | 잡기 |
| Grasping | *jaba* | 잡아 |

| to Punch | *jireuda* | 지르다 |
|---|---|---|
| a Punch | *jireugi* | 지르기 |
| Punching | *jilleo* | 질러 |
| whilst Punching | *jireumyeo* | 지르며 |

There are relatively few irregular formations, and it is unlikely that you will need to know these for the purposes of Taekwondo.

# Translating Names

When speaking a foreign language, it sounds peculiar to suddenly swap to one's own language in order to say someone's name. As Korean has its own alphabet, you can write your or someone else's English name in Korean, and then use it when you are speaking Korean. You can do this easily with the information that we have just covered. However, remember that some sounds cannot be reproduced in the Korean alphabet. As English words are frequently written in the Korean alphabet, there are common ways of dealing with this.

| English Sound | f | v | th | z |
|---|---|---|---|---|
| Korean Equivalent | ㅍ | ㅂ | ㅆ | ㅈ |

There is also the problem that English names can have all kinds of consonants in them. In Korean they have difficulty with this, so tend to add the *"eu"* or *"i"* sounds so that they can pronounce the consonants as they should be.

| English Name | Jasper | David |
|---|---|---|
| Problem | would change to *jatpeu* | would become *deibit* |
| Korean Equivalent | *jaseupeu* | *deibideu* |

If you translate your full name, you must place your family name first, followed by your given name.

| English Order | John Smith | Adam Blair |
|---|---|---|
| Korean Order | Smith John | Blair Adam |

## 사
# 용어과문구

## ④
# Terminology and Phrases

# Key

You may occasionally see in this index some capital letters which follow on from the entry, these will be in ( ) rounded brackets. These mark particular words according to the key below.

| Initials | Meaning |
|---|---|
| RL | The actual translation of this means something slightly different out of context but is used anyway. |
| CT | This is the most commonly used term but perhaps not the most accurate or appropriate. |
| OT | This is the official term but is not perhaps the most accurate or appropriate. |
| PT | This is a better way of translating the word. |
| AT | This word is a synonym or an alternative phrase that can help to pinpoint the exact definition. |
| LT | This is the literal translation of a word; generally applies to compound nouns. |
| IF | This word is used predominantly with the International Taekwondo Federation. |
| WF | This word is preferred by the World Taekwondo Federation. |
| LN | There is an interesting language point with this entry |
| WA | There is a warning with this entry about its meaning of usage. |
| SS | This entry may not be relevant to the syllabus you follow but is still regarded as important for this book. |
| NK | This is an unusual North Korean variant of the word. |
| SK | This is an unusual South Korean variant of the word. |

There is also a literary key, denoting the type of word that a specific entry is which is used if there is ambiguity and is generally omitted the remainder of the time. The abbreviations are made in [ ] square brackets.

| Abbreviation | Meaning |
|---|---|

| | |
|---:|---|
| excl. | Exclamation or General Common Phrase. |
| vt. | Transitive Verb. A verb that requires an object. |
| vi. | Intransitive Verb. A verb that does not require an object, only the subject is needed. |
| n. | Noun |
| adj. | Adjective |
| adv. | Adverb |

Anything placed within { } wavy brackets is continuation information.

Most of the sections consist of two parts, one for world federation words, and the other for international federation terms. Sometimes there may be additional, general lists which are used by both or neither organisation. None of the lists are exclusive, and you can mix and match words as you choose. Don't think that you must only use words that are listed under your organisation's list; it is all one language and all equally interchangeable. Neither are they totally exhaustive; if both organisations use some words they may just be placed in one of the lists to avoid repetition.

In each table, the entries will be divided up into blocks: those with shading and those without. These blocks are designed to make manageable chunks for you to learn and so are generally kept to around twenty entries.

# Numbers and Counting

There are two counting systems in Korean: one which evolved from the older language, and the other which is native to Korean. The two systems are not always interchangeable, and each has designated parts of language with which they can be used.

A common perception is that the evolved system actual represents order rather than number: first, second, third, forth, and so on. But this is not always the case, it just happens that for ordinal situations the evolved numbers are used, but can be used as ordinary numerals as well.

The two sets of numerals may intertwine; when denoting time you use one sequence for minutes and the other for hours. There are also many phrases which require one word if you use the native Korean set, and another if you use the Sino Korean set.

# Native Numerals

The native numerals work partly in a way similar to European numerals, and partly in a way similar to Oriental ones.

Each of the numbers one to ten has a different word. Then, like English, each of the tens numbers has a different word: *twenty, thirty, forty,* and so on. These are loosely comparable to their unit words, also similar to English: *two* is alike to *twenty; three* is alike to *thirty* and so forth.

The system then works similarly to English when we want to convey more specific numbers. If I want to say *seventy-four,* I use the same method as English: the word for *seventy, ilheun,* followed by the word for *four, net,* to make *ilheunnet.*

The only difference to the English formation is that the numbers between ten and twenty do no have individual words: *eleven, twelve, thirteen, fourteen* and so on. In Korean, these numbers are formed just as the rest of them are: *ten-one, yeolhana, ten-two, yeoldul, ten-three, yeolset.*

| English | Romanisation | Hangeul | Hanja |
|---|---|---|---|
| Numbers | *sutja* | 숫자 | 數字 |
| One | *hana* | 하나 | |
| Two | *dul* | 둘 | |
| Three | *set* | 셋 | |
| Four | *net* | 넷 | |
| Five | *daseot* | 다섯 | |
| Six | *yeoseot* | 여섯 | |
| Seven | *ilgop* | 일곱 | |
| Eight | *yeodeol* | 여덟 | |

| Nine | *ahop* | 아홉 |
| Ten | *yeol* | 열 |
| Eleven | *yeolhana* | 열하나 |
| Twelve | *yeoldul* | 열둘 |
| Thirteen | *yeolset* | 열셋 |
| Twenty | *seumul* | 스물 |
| Twenty-one | *seumulhana* | 스물하나 |
| Twenty-two | *seumuldul* | 스물둘 |
| Twenty-three | *seumulset* | 스물셋 |
| Thirty | *seoreun* | 서른 |
| Forty | *maheun* | 마흔 |
| Fifty | *swin* | 쉰 |
| Sixty | *yesun* | 예순 |
| Seventy | *ilheun* | 일흔 |
| Eighty | *yeodeun* | 여든 |
| Ninety | *aheun* | 아흔 |
| Hundred | *on* | 온 |
| Thousand | *jeumeun* | 즈믄 |
| Ten-thousand, Myriad | *deumeon, gol* | 드먼 / 골 |

## Sino Numerals

The evolved numerals work in the same way as most oriental languages, and identically to Chinese.

The numbers one to ten are unique, as are each of the numbers for ten, hundred, thousand, myriad and so on. To form a multiple of these orders of magnitude, we simply place the required unit value before it: *twenty* is essentially *two-ten*, *eighty* being *eight-ten*. This is the same as our method for naming the hundreds and thousands: *three-hundred, five-thousand*. This method is extended along the whole counting system.

| English | Romanisation | Hangeul | Hanja |
|---|---|---|---|
| Zero | *gong* | 공 | |
| Zero | *yeong (NK ryeong)* | 영 (NK 령) | |
| One | *il* | 일 | 一 |
| Two | *i* | 이 | 二 |
| Three | *sam* | 삼 | 三 |
| Four | *sa* | 사 | 四 |
| Five | *o* | 오 | 五 |
| Six | *yuk (NK ryuk)* | 육 (NK 륙) | |
| Seven | *chil* | 칠 | 七 |
| Eight | *pal* | 팔 | 八 |
| Nine | *gu* | 구 | 九 |
| Ten | *ship* | 십 | 十 |
| Eleven | *shibil* | 십일 | 十一 |
| Twelve | *shibi* | 십이 | 十二 |
| Thirteen | *shipsam* | 십삼 | 十三 |
| Twenty | *iship* | 이십 | 二十 |
| Twenty-one | *ishibil* | 이십일 | 二十一 |
| Twenty-two | *ishibi* | 이십이 | 二十二 |
| Twenty-three | *ishipsam* | 이십삼 | 二十三 |
| Thirty | *samship* | 삼십 | 三十 |
| Forty | *saship* | 사십 | 四十 |
| Fifty | *oship* | 오십 | 五十 |
| Sixty | *yukship (NK ryukship)* | 육십 (NK 륙십) | 十 |
| Seventy | *chilship* | 칠십 | 七十 |
| Eighty | *palship* | 팔십 | 八十 |

| Nintey | *guship* | 구십 | 九十 |
| Hundred | *baek* | 백 | 百 |
| Thousand | *cheon* | 천 | 千 |
| Ten-thousand, Myriad | *man* | 만 | 萬 |

# General Vocabulary

We now come across examples of Korean nouns. In English we have both a singular and a plural form of every noun. This is typically the addition of an *s* to the end of the word. In Korean however, like many eastern languages, the same word is used for both the singular and the plural; there is no distinction.

| **English** | **Romanisation** | **Hangeul** | **Hanja** |
| --- | --- | --- | --- |
| Martial Arts | *musul* | 무술 | 武術 |
| Strike with the Foot | *tae* | 태 | 跆 |
| Strike with the Hand | *gwon* | 권 | 拳 |
| Way of Life | *do* | 도 | 道 |
| Way of the Foot and Hand, Taekwondo | *taegwondo* | 태권도 | 跆拳道 |
| The Chang Heon School | *changheonyu* | 창헌유 | |
| Taekwondo History | *taegwondo yeoksa* | 태권도 역사 | |
| Taekwondo Composition | *taegwondo guseong* | 태권도 구성 | 跆拳道 構成 |
| Cycle of Taekwondo, Circle of Taekwondo, Circle of the Way | *sunhwan do* | 순환 도 | 循環 道 |
| Choi Hong Hi | *choihonghui* | 최홍희 | 崔泓熙 |

| | | | |
|---|---|---|---|
| The Orient | *dong-yang* | 동양 | 東洋 |
| Founder | *seollipja* | 설립자 | 設立者 |
| Education, Training | *gyoyuk* | 교육 | 教育 |
| Course (AT Series of Lessons), Curriculum | *gyogwa gwajeong* | 교과과정 | 教科課程 |
| Syllabus | *gaeyo* | 개요 | 概要 |
| Theory | *iron* | 이론 | 理論 |
| Thesis | *nonmun* | 논문 | 論文 |
| Essay | *jangmun* | 장문 | 長文 |
| Grammar | *munbeop* | 문법 | 文法 |
| Vocabulary | *eohwi* | 어휘 | 語彙 |
| Ability | *neungnyeok* | 능력 | |
| Age | *nai* | 나이 | |
| Gender | *seong* | 성 | 性 |
| Nationality | *gukjeok* | 국적 | 國籍 |
| Name | *ireum* | 이름 | |
| Easy | *swiun* | 쉬운 | |
| Difficult | *himdeun* | 힘든 | |
| Elite [adj.] | *jeong-yeui* | 정예의 | |
| Documentation | *seoryu* | 서류 | 書類 |
| Official Terms | *wanseong jejeong-yong-eo* | 완성 제정용어 | |
| Association | *danchehyeophoe* | 단체협회 | 團體協會 |
| Federation | *yeonmaeng* | 연맹 | 聯盟 |
| Union | *yeonhap* | 연합 | 聯合 |
| South Korea | *han-guk* | 한국 | 韓國 |
| North Korea | *bukhan* | 북한 | 北韓 |
| Traditional | *jeontongjeogin* | 전통적인 | |

| | | | |
|---|---|---|---|
| Tradition | *jeontong* | 전통 | 傳統 |
| Custom / Tradition | *gwansup* | 관습 | 慣習 |
| Scroll | *durumari* | 두루마리 | |
| Banner | *gi* | 기 | 旗 |
| Confucianism | *yugyo* | 유교 | 儒敎 |
| Confucius | *gongja* | 공자 | 孔子 |
| Culture | *munhwa* | 문화 | 文化 |
| Buddhism | *bulgyo* | 불교 | 佛敎 |
| Buddhist [n.] | *bulgyoshinja* | 불교신자 | 佛敎信者 |
| Buddhist [adj.] | *bulgyoui* | 불교의 | |
| Buddhist Meditation | *chamseon* | 참선 | 參禪 |
| Ceremony | *shik / uishik* | 식/의식 | 式/儀式 |
| Legend | *jeonseol* | 전설 | 傳說 |
| Legacy | *yusan* | 유산 | 遺産 |
| Attack [n.] | *gonggyeok* | 공격 | 攻擊 |
| Defence | *bang-eo* | 방어 | 防禦 |
| Technique | *gisul* | 기술 | 技術 |
| Essential Technique | *juyogi* | 주요기 | 主要基 |
| Attack Technique | *gonggyeokgi* | 공격기 | 攻擊基 |
| Defence Technique | *bang-eogi* | 방어기 | 防禦基 |
| Hand Technique | *sugi* | 수기 | |
| Foot Technique | *jokgi* | 족기 | |
| Theory of Power | *himui wonni* | 힘의 원리 | |
| Reaction Force | *bandongnyeok* | 반동력 | 反動力 |
| Concentration | *jipjung* | 집중 | 集中 |
| Equilibrium | *gyunhyeong* | 균형 | 均衡 |
| Breathing | *hoheup* | 호흡 | 呼吸 |

| | | | |
|---|---|---|---|
| Speed | *sokdo* | 속도 | 速度 |
| Meditation | *mungnyeom* | 묵념 | 默念 |
| Force, Power | *him* | 힘 | |
| Energy, Essence | *gi* | 기 | 氣 |
| Yell with Concentration | *gihap* | 기합 | 氣合 |
| Mind, Spirit | *ma-eum* | 마음 | |
| Reflex, Reaction | *baneung* | 반응 | 反應 |
| Breath Control | *hoheup jojeol* | 호흡 조절 | 呼吸 調節 |

# Clothing, Training and Lessons

## Clothing and General Training

In this section I have included some vocabulary for traditional Korean clothing. These words would never be used to describe your training clothes as they refer to very specific styles of dress.

The *hanbok* is the conventional formal wear for Koreans which was worn regularly by the aristocracy of ancient Korea. It is readily identifiable by the wide sleeves and lends numerous design elements to the modern *dobok*. The *hanbok* can often be seen in Korea today at important historical or culture events or locations, and in particular at weddings. If you were attending a highly formal Taekwondo event, such as a notable competition or grading, then you might choose to acquire and wear one.

| English | Romanisation | Hangeul | Hanja |
|---|---|---|---|
| Training Hall | *dojang* | 도장 | 道場 |
| Flag | *gukgi* | 국기 | 國旗 |
| Uniform (General) | *gyobok* | 교복 | 校服 |
| Uniform (RL Clothing of the | *dobok* | 도복 | 道服 |

| | | | |
|---|---|---|---|
| Way) {Taekwondo} | | | |
| Belt | *tti* | 띠 | |
| Training Suit Shirt / Jacket | *jeogori, sang-i* | 저고리, 상이 | |
| Training Suit Trousers | *baji, hai* | 바지, 하이 | |
| Traditional Dress | *jeontong-ot* | 전통옷 | |
| Traditional Korean Clothes | *hanbok* | 한복 | 韓服 |

# Belts and Ranks

In oriental languages it is common to have measure words. Measure words allow one to quantify nouns. In English we can say that we have *three certificates*, there is already an idea of quantity here. However in Korean word we would need a measure word in between that might roughly translate as *sheets*, making *three sheets of certificates*. We do occasionally have a similar situation in English, for example *two bunches of flowers* where *bunches* gives a new idea of measurement to the phrase.

The topic of Korean measure words is for the most part irrelevant to Taekwondo, except for when talking about belts, because colours also demand a measure word. As you can see in the table, the different colours of belts have a root word, which informs us which colour we are talking about, followed by the measure word for colour "*saek*". You should include this word when talking about colours of belts.

| **English** | **Romanisation** | **Hangeul** | **Hanja** |
|---|---|---|---|
| System of Rank {Specific to Martial Arts} | *dangeup jedo* | 단급제도 | |
| Junior Rank {Colour Belt} | *geup* | 급 | |
| Senior Rank {Black Belt} | *dan* | 단 | |
| White Belt | *hayan tti, hansaek tti,* | 하얀띠, | 白色 |

|  | huin tti, huinsaek tti, baeksaek tti | 힌색띠, 흰띠, 흰색 띠, 백색띠 |  |
|---|---|---|---|
| Yellow Belt | noran tti, noransaek tti | 노란띠, 노란색 띠 |  |
| Orange Belt | juhwang tti, juhwangsaek tti | 주황띠, 주황색 띠 |  |
| Green Belt | nok tti, noksaek tti | 녹띠, 녹색띠 |  |
| Purple Belt | bora tti | 보라띠 |  |
| Blue Belt | paran tti, paransaek tti, cheong tti, cheongsaek tti | 파란띠, 파란색 띠, 청띠, 청색 띠 |  |
| Red Belt | ppalgan tti, ppalgansaek tti | 빨간띠, 빨간색 띠 |  |
| Brown Belt | nuran tti | 누런띠 |  |
| Bodan / Poom Belt | bodan tti, pum tti | 보단띠, 품띠 |  |
| Black Belt | geomjeong tti, geomjeongsaek tti, heuk tti, heuksaek tti | 검정띠, 검정색 띠, 흑띠, 흑색 띠 |  |

## Activities and Lessons

| English | Romanisation | Hangeul | Hanja |
|---|---|---|---|
| Training | dallyeon | 단련 | 鍛鍊 |
| Exercise | yeonseup, undong | 연습, 운동 | 演習, 練習, 鍊習 |
| Practice | suryeon | 수련 | 修鍊, 修練 |
| Lesson | sueop | 수업 | 受業 |
| Training Schedule | shiganpyo | 시간표 | 時間表 |

| English | Romanization | Hangul | Hanja |
|---|---|---|---|
| Motion, Movement, Exercise | *undong* | 운동 | |
| Pattern | *hyeong, teul, pumsae* | 형, 틀, 품새 | 型, 品勢 |
| Breaking | *gyeokpa* | 격파 | 擊破 |
| Stretching | *pyeogi* | 펴기 | |
| Free Training | *dosu dallyeon* | 도수단련 | 徒手鍛鍊 |
| Fundamental Exercise | *gibon suryeon* | 기본 수련 | 基本 修鍊, 基本 修練 |
| Practice Method | *suryeon beop* | 수련법 | 修鍊/修練 法 |
| Exercise Method | *yeonseup beop* | 연습 법 | 演習/練習/鍊習 法 |
| Practice-Leading Methods, Class-Leading Procedure | *suryeon jido beop* | 수련 지도 법 | 修鍊/修練 指導 法 |
| Method of Application | *sayong beop* | 사용법 | 使用法 |
| Pattern Direction Diagram | *banghyang pyo* | 방향표 | |
| Side View | *yeop moseup* | 옆모습 | |
| Front View | *ap moseup* | 앞모습 | |
| Back View | *dwi moseup* | 뒤모습 | |
| Application, Usage | *sayong* | 사용 | 使用 |
| Press-Up, Push-Up | *momtong batchigi* | 몸통 받치기 | |
| Forearm to Forearm Knocking Exercise | *palmok dae palmok* | 팔목 대 팔목 | |
| Warm-Up, Preparation | *junbi undong* | 준비 운동 | 準備運動 |
| Warm-Down | *jeongni undong* | 정리 운동 | 運動 |
| to be Barefoot | *maenbarida* | 맨발이다 | |
| Feedback | *pideubaek* | 피드백 | |
| Silence [n.] | *goyo* | 고요 | |

| | | |
|---|---|---|
| Question [n.] | *jilmun* | 질문 |
| Answer [n.] | *dap* | 답 |
| to Assist | *dopda* | 돕다 |
| to Assign a Task (RL to Give) | *juda* | 주다 |
| Class of Students | *hakgeup* | 학급 |
| Advice | *cho-eon* | 초언 |
| Absent-Minded | *meonghan* | 멍한 |
| to Relieve, to Take Over from | *gyodae hada* | 교대하다 |
| Moral, Message, School Motto | *gyohun* | 교훈 |

# Forms

Some people refer to forms as patterns, but as form is a more generally understood term in martial arts, because many other martial arts refer to them as forms, this is perhaps the better word to use. Many forms also have no repetition, so pattern seems incorrect.

| English | Romanisation | Hangeul | Hanja |
|---|---|---|---|
| Form, Pattern | *teul* | 틀 | |
| Form, Pattern | *pumsae* | 품새 | 品勢 |
| Form, Pattern | *hyeong* | 형 | 型 / 形 |

## WTF

| English | Romanisation | Hangeul | Hanja |
|---|---|---|---|
| Kicho 1 (RL Foundation 1) | *gicho il jang* | 기초 일장 | 基礎一場 |

| Kicho 2 (RL Foundation 2) | gicho i jang | 기초 이장 | 基礎二場 |
| --- | --- | --- | --- |
| Taegeuk 1 {Heaven and Yang} | taegeuk il jang | 태극 일장 | 太極一場 |
| Taegeuk 2 {Firmness and Softness} | taegeuk i jang | 태극 이장 | 太極二場 |
| Taegeuk 3 {Hot and Bright} | taegeuk sam jang | 태극 삼장 | 太極三場 |
| Taegeuk 4 {Thunder} | taegeuk sa jang | 태극 사장 | 太極四場 |
| Taegeuk 5 {Wind} | taegeuk o jang | 태극 오장 | 太極五場 |
| Taegeuk 6 {Water} | taegeuk yuk jang | 태극 육장 | 太極六場 |
| Taegeuk 7 {Mountain} | taegeuk chil jang | 태극 칠장 | 太極七場 |
| Taegeuk 8 {Earth and Yin} | taegeuk pal jang | 태극 팔장 | 太極八場 |
| Go-Ryeo | goryeo | 고려 | |
| Geum-Gang | geumgang | 금강 | |
| Tae-Baek | taebaek | 태백 | |
| Pyeong-Won | pyeong-won | 평원 | |
| Ship-Jin | shipjin | 십진 | |
| Ji-Tae | jitae | 지태 | |
| Cheon-Gwon | cheon-gwon | 천권 | |
| Han-Su | hansu | 한수 | |
| Ir-Yeo | iryeo | 일여 | |

# ITF

Due to the highly customised nature of the international federation's syllabus, you may use some patterns and not others, and you may also have additional variations of the exercises.

| English | Romanisation | Hangeul | Hanja |
|---|---|---|---|
| Four Directional Punch Variation 1 (RL Four Pillars) | saju jireugi il | 사주 지르기 일 | 四柱 |
| Four Directional Punch Variation 2 (RL Four Pillars) | saju jireugi i | 사주 지르기 이 | 四柱 |
| Four Directional Block (RL Four Pillars) | saju makgi | 사주 막기 | 四柱 |
| Cheon-Ji | cheonji | 천지 | 天地 |
| Dan-Gun | dan-gun | 단군 | 檀君 |
| Do-San | dosan | 도산 | 島山 |
| Won-Hyo | wonhyo | 원효 | 元曉 |
| Yul-Gok | yulgok | 율곡 | 栗谷 |
| Jung-Geun | junggeun | 중근 | 重根 |
| Toi-Gye | toigye | 퇴계 | 退溪 |
| Hwa-Rang | hwarang | 화랑 | 花郎 |
| Chung-Mu | chungmu | 충무 | 忠武 |
| Gwang-Ge | gwangge | 광개 | 廣開 |
| Po-Eun | po-eun | 포은 | 圃隱 |
| Gye-Baek | gyebaek | 계백 | 階伯 |
| Ui-Am | uiam | 의암 | 義菴 |
| Chung-Jang | chungjang | 충장 | 忠壯 |
| Go-Dang | godang | 고당 | 古堂 |
| Sam-Il | samil | 삼일 | 三一 |
| Yu-Shin | yushin | 유신 | 庾信 |
| Choe-Yeong | choeyeong | 최영 | 崔瑩 |
| Yeon-Gae | yeon-gae | 연개 | 淵蓋 |
| Eul-Ji | eulji | 을지 | 乙支 |

| | | | |
|---|---|---|---|
| Mun-Mu | *munmu* | 문무 | 文武 |
| Seo-San | *seosan* | 서산 | 西山 |
| Se-Jong | *sejong* | 세종 | 世宗 |
| Tong-Il | *tong-il* | 통일 | 統一 |
| Ju-Che (RL Self Reliance) | *juche* | 주체 | 主體 |

# Sparring

## WTF

| English | Romanisation | Hangeul |
|---|---|---|
| Sparring | *gyeorugi* | 겨루기 |
| Select Sparring / Set Sparring | *gyeorugi ui jongnyu* | 겨루기 의 종류 |
| Three-Step Middle Defence Sparring {Body} | *sebeon gyeorugi (momtong)* | 세번 겨루기 (몸통) |
| Three-Step High Defence Sparring {Face} | *sebeon gyeorugi (eolgul)* | 세번 겨루기 (얼굴) |
| One-Step Middle Defence Sparring {Body} | *hanbeon gyeorugi (momtong)* | 한번 겨루기 (몸통) |
| One-Step High Defence Sparring {Face} | *hanbeon gyeorugi (eolgul)* | 한번 겨루기(얼굴) |
| Floor Defence Sparring (PT Sitting on Floor Sparring) | *anja gyeorugi* | 앉아 겨루기 |
| Seated Defence Sparring (RL Chair | *uija gyeorugi* | 의자 겨루기 |

| Sparring) | | |
|---|---|---|
| Short Club Defence Sparring | *jjalbeun makdae gyeorugi* | 짧은 막대 겨루기 |
| Long Bar Defence Sparring | *gin makdae gyeorugi* | 긴 막대 겨루기 |
| Knife Defence Sparring | *jjalbeun kal gyeorugi* | 짧은 칼 겨루기 |
| Sword Defence Sparring | *gin kal gyeorugi* | 긴 칼 겨루기 |
| Pistol Defence Sparring | *gwonchong gyeorugi* | 권총 겨루기 |
| Rifle & Bayonet Defence Sparring | *chonggeom gyeorugi* | 총검 겨루기 |

# ITF

As you can undoubtedly see in the table, there are three words for sparring that are used by various factions of the international taekwondo federation and its closely related styles. The most commonly used word is *"matseogi"* though this actually does not mean *sparring*. The first two words, *gyeorugi* and *daeryeon* completely refer to the act of sparring as in practice fighting, whereas *matseogi* literally means *to stand in opposition*, hence matseogi can refer to real and practice sparring.

| **English** | **Romanisation** | **Hangeul** |
|---|---|---|
| Sparring | *gyeorugi* | 겨루기 |
| Sparring | *daeryeon* | 대련 |
| Sparring | *matseogi* | 맞서기 |
| Free Sparring | *jayu daeryeon* | 자유대련 |
| Semi-Free Sparring | *banjayu daeryeon* | 반자유대련 |
| Set Sparring | *yaksok daeryeon* | 약속 대련 |
| One Step Sparring | *il bo daeryeon* | 일보대련 |
| Two Step Sparring | *i bo daeryeon* | 이보대련 |

| | | |
|---|---|---|
| Three Step Sparring | *sam bo daeryeon* | 삼보대련 |
| Traditional Sparring | *jeontong daeryeon* | 전통대련 |
| Model (AT Example) Sparring | *mobeom matseogi* | 모범 맞서기 |
| Against Weapons | *dae mugi* | 대무기 |
| Against Sudden Attack | *dae bulshi gonggyeok* | 대불시공격 |
| Flexible Guarding Posture | *jase byeonhwa* | 자세변화 |
| Demonstration | *shiwi* | 시위 |
| Feint | *giman* | 기만 |

| English | Romanisation | Hangeul |
|---|---|---|
| Self-Defence | *hoshin* | 호신 |
| Self-Defence Techniques | *hoshinsul* | 호신술 |
| Stability, Composure | *anjeong* | 안정 |
| Dynamic (AT Kinetic) Stability | *dongjeok anjeong* | 동적안정 |
| Static Stability | *jeongjeok anjeong* | 정적안정 |

# Competitions, Examinations and Events

In this section we have an excellent example of an English word being assimilated into the Korean alphabet. The word *medal* in English becomes exactly the same "*medal*" in Korean.

| English | Romanisation | Hangeul | Hanja |
|---|---|---|---|
| Competition | *gyeongjaeng, gyeonggi* | 경쟁, 경기 | 競爭, 競技 |
| Rules | *gyujeong* | 규정 | 規定 |

| Medal | medal | 메달 | |
|---|---|---|---|
| Tournament | shihap | 시합 | |
| to Compete | gyeongjaenghada | 경쟁하다 | |
| Jury | baeshim | 배심 | 陪審 |
| Referee | jushim | 주심 | 主審 |
| Judge | bushim | 부심 | 副審 |
| Timer | gyeshim | 계심 | |
| Recorder | girok | 기록 | 記錄 |
| Caller | sorihishim | 소리치심 | |
| Umpire | shimpanwon | 심판원 | 審判員 |
| Refereeing or Umpiring | shimpan | 심판 | 審判 |
| Competitor | gyeongjaengja | 경쟁자 | |
| Protective Gear | hogu | 호구 | |
| Protective Cup | nangshim hogu | 낭심호구 | |
| Chest Protector | gaseum hogu | 가슴호구 | |
| 1st Round | il hoejeon | 일회전 | 一會戰 |
| 2nd Round | i hoejeon | 이회전 | 二會戰 |
| 3rd Round | sam hoejeon | 삼회전 | 三會戰 |
| Blue | cheong | 청 | 青 |
| Red | hong | 홍 | 紅 |
| Versus, Against | dae | 대 | |
| Male [n.] | namja | 남자 | 男子 |
| Female [n.] | yeoja | 여자 | 女子 |
| Weight | chegeup | 체급 | 體級 |
| Height | shinjang | 신장 | 身長 |
| Time Allowance | shigan baedang | 시간 배당 | 時間 配當 |
| Injury | busang | 부상 | 負傷 |

| English | Romanisation | Hangeul | Hanja |
|---|---|---|---|
| Disqualification | shilgyeok | 실격 | 失格 |
| Foul | banchik | 반칙 | 反則 |
| Warning | gyeonggo | 경고 | 警告 |
| Demerit (AT Points Removed) | gamjeom | 감점 | 減點 |
| Merit (AT Points Added) | deukjeom | 득점 | 得點 |
| Scoring | chaejeom | 채점 | 採點 |
| Pre-Warning (AT Notice) | juui | 주의 | |

| English | Romanisation | Hangeul | Hanja |
|---|---|---|---|
| Examination, Inspection | shimsa | 심사 | 審査 |
| Candidate | eungshija | 응시자 | 應試者 |
| Examination | shiheom | 시험 | 試驗 |
| Examiner | shiheomgwan | 시험관 | 試驗官 |
| Requirement | jogeon | 조건 | 條件 |
| Proceedings | haengsa | 행사 | 行事 |
| Qualification | jagyeok | 자격 | 資格 |
| Demonstration, Example | shibeom | 시범 | 示範 |
| Demonstration | gwashi | 과시 | 誇示 |

# Equipment

Much of the apparatus listed here has fallen out of use in Taekwondo, sometimes because individual instructors cannot afford it or because newer methods are being used. A lot of this apparatus can be constructed from simple materials, as per the original intention.

| English | Romanisation | Hangeul |
|---|---|---|
| Equipment | *jangbi* | 장비 |
| Apparatus, Framework | *teul* | 틀 |
| Brick | *byeokdol* | 벽돌 |
| Board | *panja* | 판자 |
| Forging Post / Pillar | *dallyeon ju* | 단련 주 |
| Post | *dae* | 대 |
| Pad | *begae* | 베개 |
| Straw Pad | *iljip begae* | 밀짚베개 |
| Sponge Pad | *seuponji begae* | 스폰지 베개 |
| Forging Pendulum | *dallyeon geune* | 단련그네 |
| Dumbbell | *aryeong* | 아령 |
| Punching Ball | *dallyeon gong* | 단련공 |
| Wooden Horse | *mokma* | 목마 |
| Jar | *danji* | 단지 |
| Sandbox | *moraetong* | 모래통 |
| Mirror | *geoul* | 거울 |
| Breaker-Board Holder | *gyeokpa teul* | 격파틀 |
| Blocking Apparatus | *makgi teul* | 막기틀 |
| Stance Apparatus | *seogi teul* | 서기틀 |
| Ankle Board | *balmok teul* | 발목틀 |
| Fixed Type | *gojeongshik* | 고정식 |
| Moveable Type | *idongshik* | 이동식 |

# Virtues and Morality

Every proper martial art has a strong moral code that comes with it. Taekwondo is noted for its even greater emphasis on the moral grounding, as is the advantage of a modern martial art. The original five virtues are listed here, as well as those of Hwarangdo, from which the Taekwondo virtues are derived, along with other useful words on the subject.

| English | Romanisation | Hangeul | Hanja |
|---|---|---|---|
| Mentality, Morality | *jeongshin* | 정신 | 精神 |
| Morality of the Way | *dodeok* | 도덕 | 道德 |
| Guiding Principle | *jichim* | 지침 | 指針 |
| Moral / Mental Culture | *suyang* | 수양 | 修養 |
| Philosophy | *cheolhak* | 철학 | 哲學 |
| Virtue | *mideok* | 미덕 | 美德 |
| Courtesy | *yejeol, yeui, uirye* | 예절, 예의, 의례 | 禮節, 禮儀, 儀禮 |
| Integrity | *jeong-ui, yeomchi, jeongjik* | 정의, 염치, 정직 | 正義, 廉恥, 正直 |
| Perseverance | *chameulseong, innae* | 참을성, 인내 | 一性, 忍耐 |
| Self Control | *jaje, geukgi* | 자제, 극기 | 自制, 克己 |
| Indomitable Spirit | *gulhajianneun-giun, baekjeolbulgul* | 굴하지않는 기운, 백절불굴 | 百折不屈 |
| Loyalty | *chungseong, chungjeol* | 충성, 충절 | 忠誠, 忠節 |
| Discipline | *hunnyeon* | 훈련 | 訓練 |
| Determination, Resolution | *gyeolshim* | 결심 | 決心 |
| Responsibility | *uimu* | 의무 | 義務 |
| Modesty | *gyeomson* | 겸손 | 謙遜, 謙巽 |
| Patience | *innae* | 인내 | 忍耐 |
| Respect | *jon-gyeong* | 존경 | 尊敬 |
| Confidence | *shinnyeom* | 신념 | 信念 |

| | | | |
|---|---|---|---|
| Concentration | *jipjung* | 집중 | 集中 |
| Peace, Harmony | *pyeonghwa* | 평화 | 平和 |
| Obedience | *sunjong* | 순종 | 順從 |
| Faith of Certain Victory | *pilseung* | 필승 | 必勝 |
| Community Service | *sahoebongsa* | 사회봉사 | 社會奉仕 |
| Humanity, Compassion | *inganae* | 인간애 | 人間愛 |
| Justice, Impartiality | *gongjeong* | 공정 | 公正 |
| Wisdom | *jihye* | 지혜 | 智慧, 知慧 |
| Trust [n.] | *shinyong* | 신용 | 信用 |
| Courage | *yonggi* | 용기 | 勇氣 |
| Awareness | *inshik* | 인식 | 認識 |
| Agile | *chaeppareun* | 채빠른 | |
| Conduct, Behaviour | *haeng-wi* | 행위 | 行爲 |
| Ethics | *yunni* | 윤리 | 倫理 |
| Respectful | *jon-gyeonghaneun* | 존경하는 | |
| Power | *him* | 힘 | |
| Morality | *dodeokseong* | 도덕성 | |
| Excellence (LT Flying above Others) | *ttwieonam* | 뛰어남 | |
| Discipline | *gyuyul* | 규율 | 規律 |
| Dedication | *jeonnyeom* | 전념 | 專念 |

The word *tenet* is frequently used when denoting virtues in Taekwondo, however this word has stronger relations to religious or spiritual guiding principals, and is therefore not as appropriate for Taekwondo, which has only mild connections to Buddhism and Confucianism.

# Nominalised Verbs

These can also be viewed as actions or action nouns. These are nouns which are formed from their corresponding verbs.

The nominalised verbs represent the foundation words of each movement name. Each word here is an action, which can have various adjectives added to make it more specific and to create a movement name. For convenience, all of these words have been placed together.

| English | Romanisation | Hangeul |
|---|---|---|
| Punch | *jireugi* | 지르기 |
| Stance | *seogi* | 서기 |
| Block | *makgi* | 막기 |
| Kick | *chagi* | 차기 |
| Sparring | *gyeorugi* | 겨루기 |
| Grasp (RL Catch) | *japgi* | 잡기 |
| Strike, Thrash | *ttaerigi* | 때리기 |
| Dodging | *pihagi* | 피하기 |
| Jumping | *ttwigi* | 뛰기 |

# WTF

| English | Romanisation | Hangeul |
|---|---|---|
| Thrust, Poke | *jjireugi* | 찌르기 |
| Strike | *chigi* | 치기 |
| Pull | *kkeulgi* | 끌기 |
| Release, Retraction | *ppaegi* | 빼기 |

# ITF

| English | Romanisation | Hangeul |
|---|---|---|
| Sparring | *daeryeon* | 대련 |
| Sparring | *matseogi* | 맞서기 |
| Checking | *meomchugi* | 멈추기 |
| Covering | *garigi* | 가리기 |
| Pressing | *nureugi* | 누르기 |
| Body Dropping | *mom natchugi* | 몸 낮추기 |
| Falling, Dropping | *natchugi* | 낮추기 |
| Movement | *omgigi* | 옮기기 |
| Step | *didigi* | 디디기 |
| Moving Step | *omgyeo didigi* | 옮겨디디기 |
| Throwing | *deonjigi* | 던지기 |
| Stretching | *pyeogi* | 펴기 |
| Thrust | *ttulgi* | 뚫기 |
| Stamp | *bapgi* | 밟기 |
| Rise | *olligi* | 올리기 |
| Forward Movement | *nagagi* | 나가기 |
| Backward Movement | *deureoogi* | 들어오기 |
| Slide | *mikkeureojigi* | 미끄러지기 |
| Falling | *tteoreojigi* | 떨어지기 |
| Holding | *batchigi* | 받치기 |
| Cross Cutting | *geotgi* | 걷기 |
| Special Technique | *teukgi* | 특기 |
| Motion {General} | *gagi* | 가기 |

# Body Parts and Critical Points

This section is a combination of general body parts words and those words which refer to the specific weak target points on the body, which not every style uses as a basis for their movements but they are still important. There is also a mixture of both technical scientific terms and everyday language.

| English | Romanisation | Hangeul |
|---|---|---|
| Body | *mom* | 몸 |
| Figure, Physique | *mommae* | 몸매 |
| Physique, Build | *chegyek* | 체격 |
| Upper Half of the Body | *sangbanshin* | 상반신 |
| Lower Half of the Body | *habanshin* | 하반신 |
| Upper Part | *sangbang* | 상방 |
| Lower Part | *habang* | 하방 |
| Critical Points | *geupso* | 급소 |
| Anatomy | *haebuhak* | 해부학 |
| Shoulder | *eokkae* | 어깨 |
| Chest | *gaseum* | 가슴 |
| Back | *deung* | 등 |
| Solar Plexus | *myeongchi* | 명치 |
| Sternum | *hyunggol* | 흉골 |
| Collar Bone (Clavicle) | *swaegol* | 쇄골 |
| Abdomen | *bokbu* | 복부 |
| Upper Abdomen (Epigastrium) | *sangbokbu* | 상복부 |
| Lower Abdomen (Hypogastrium) | *habokbu* | 하복부 |
| Heart | *shimjang* | 심장 |
| Spleen | *bijang* | 비장 |
| Liver | *gan, ganjang* | 간, 간장 |

| | | |
|---|---|---|
| Groin | *sataguni, garang-i, saet* | 사타구니, 가랑이, 샡 |
| Kidneys | *kongpat, shinjang* | 콩팥, 신장 |
| Rib | *neukgol* | 늑골 |
| Floating Rib | *budong neukgol* | 부동늑골 |
| Lower Abdomen | *danjeon* | 단전 |
| Upper Back (RL Scapula, Shoulder Blade) | *gyeon-gap* | 견갑 |
| Small of the Back | *gyeongchu* | 경추 |
| Coccyx | *migol* | 미골 |
| Organ | *jujik* | 주직 |
| Tendon | *shimjul* | 심줄 |
| Sinew | *himjul* | 힘줄 |
| Artery | *dongmaek* | 동맥 |
| Vein | *jeongmaek* | 정맥 |
| Muscle | *geunyuk* | 근육 |
| Bone | *ppyeo* | 뼈 |
| Ligament | *indae* | 인대 |
| Joint | *gwanjeol* | 관절 |
| Head | *meori* | 머리 |
| Face | *eolgul* | 얼굴 |
| Eye | *nun* | 눈 |
| Nose | *ko* | 코 |
| Jaw, Chin | *teok* | 턱 |
| Ear | *gwi* | 귀 |
| Neck | *mok* | 목 |
| Throat | *mokgumeong* | 목구멍 |
| Forehead | *ima* | 이마 |
| Occiput (Back of | *hudu* | 후두 |

| Head) | | |
|---|---|---|
| Skull | *dugaegol* | 두개골 |
| Temple | *gwanjanori* | 관자놀이 |
| Bridge of Nose | *konmaru* | 콧마루 |
| Centre of the Forehead | *migan* | 미간 |
| Eyeball | *angu, nunal* | 안구, 눈알 |
| Philtrum | *injung* | 인중 |
| Lips | *ipsul* | 입술 |
| Windpipe | *sumtong* | 숨통 |
| Jaw | *teok* | 턱 |
| Side Jaw | *yeopteok* | 옆턱 |
| Jaw Point | *mitteok* | 밑턱 |
| Eyelid | *angeom* | 안검 |
| Eye | *anbu* | 안부 |
| Neck Artery | *mokdongmaek* | 목동맥 |
| Upper Neck | *wimok* | 위목 |
| Adam's Apple | *gyeolhu* | 결후 |
| Chin | *teok* | 턱 |
| Arm | *pal* | 팔 |
| Forearm | *palmok* | 팔목 |
| Elbow | *palgup, palkkumchi* | 팔굽, 팔꿈치 |
| Biceps | *idugeun, parui altong* | 이두근, 팔의알통 |
| Triceps | *samdugeun* | 삼두근 |
| Armpit | *gyeodeurang* | 겨드랑 |
| Elbow Joint | *palmok gwanjeol* | 팔목관절 |
| Hand | *son* | 손 |
| Palm | *sonbadak* | 손바닥 |
| Finger | *songarak* | 손가락 |

| Fingertip | *sonkkeut* | 손끝 |
| Wrist | *sonmok* | 손목 |
| Inner Wrist | *ansonmok* | 안손목 |
| Leg | *dari* | 다리 |
| Knee | *mureup* | 무릎 |
| Hollow of the Knee | *ogeum* | 오금 |
| Shin | *jeonggang-i* | 정강이 |
| Thigh | *neoljeokdari* | 넓적다리 |
| Groin | *nangshim, sataguni* | 낭심, 사타구니 |
| Hip | *eongdeong* | 엉덩 |
| Leg Joint | *dari gwanjeol* | 다리 관절 |
| Calf | *jangttanji* | 장딴지 |
| Inner Thigh | *chibu* | 치부 |
| Tibia (CT Shin) | *gyeonggol* | 경골 |
| Inner Tibia | *angyeonggol* | 안경골 |
| Back Tibia | *dwitgyeonggol* | 뒷경골 |
| Outer Tibia | *bakkat gyeonggol* | 바깥경골 |
| Foot Point | *balkkeut* | 발끝 |
| Toe | *balgarak* | 발가락 |
| Foot | *bal* | 발 |
| Ball of Foot | *ap kkumchi* | 앞꿈치 |
| Heel | *dwi kkumchi* | 뒤꿈치 |
| Ankle | *balmok* | 발목 |
| Instep | *baldeung* | 발등 |
| Achilles Heel | *dwichuk yakjeom* | 뒤축 약점 |

# Striking Surfaces and Hand Formations

This section deals with words that describe what you are striking with, rather than the target that you are striking. The words listed in this book are the modern Korean words, which typically do not have any Hanja relatives. There is also a second set of older words which aren't in use much anymore, and are unsurprisingly limited in their capacity to describe movements, thus they have not been included.

## WTF

The world federation's words for this category are quite difficult to pronounce, this is an occasion where perhaps a sharing of terminology is fitting.

| English | Romanisation | Hangeul |
|---|---|---|
| Fist | *gwon* | 권 |
| Fist | *jumeok* | 주먹 |
| Standing Fist | *se-un jumeok* | 세운주먹 |
| Inverted Fist | *jeothin jumeok* | 젖힌주먹 |
| Back Fist | *deung jumeok* | 등주먹 |
| Hammer Fist | *me jumeok* | 메주먹 |
| Flat Fist | *pyeon jumeok* | 편주먹 |
| Knuckle Fist | *soseum jumeok* | 솟음주먹 |
| Pincer Fist | *jipge jumeok* | 집게주먹 |
| Knuckles {First Row} | *cheot madi* | 첫마디 |
| Knuckles {Second Row} | *duljjae madi* | 둘째마디 |
| Knuckles {Last Before Tips} | *setjjae madi* | 셋째마디 |

| English | Romanisation | Hangeul |
|---|---|---|
| Thumb | *eomji songarak* | 엄지손가락 |
| Forefinger | *jipge songarak* | 집게손가락 |
| Middle Finger | *gaunde songarak* | 가운데손가락 |
| Ring Finger | *mumyeongji songarak* | 무명지손가락 |
| Little Finger | *saekki songarak* | 새끼손가락 |
| Finger Tips | *sonkkeut* | 손끝 |
| Blade of Hand | *sonnal* | 손날 |
| Blade of Hand {Thumb Side} | *sonnaldeung* | 손날등 |
| Palm Heel | *batangson* | 바탕손 |
| Arc Hand, Crescent Hand | *agwison, bandalson* | 아귀손, 반달손 |
| Palm Heel Hand | *jangkal* | 장칼 |
| Rake Hand | *galgwi son* | 갈귀손 |
| Upper Elbow | *ap palkkum* | 앞팔꿈 |
| Back Elbow | *dwi palkkum* | 뒤팔꿈 |
| Side Elbow | *yeop palkkum* | 옆팔꿈 |
| Downward Elbow | *naeryeo palkkum* | 내려팔꿈 |
| Ball of Foot | *ap juk* | 앞죽 |
| Heel Bottom | *dwi juk* | 뒤죽 |
| Blade of Foot | *bannal* | 발날 |
| Arch of Foot | *bannal deung* | 발날등 |
| Shin | *jeonggang-i* | 정강이 |
| Calf | *jangttanji* | 장딴지 |

# ITF

| English | Romanisation | Hangeul |
|---|---|---|

| | | |
|---|---|---|
| Hand Parts | *sangbanshin* | 상반신 |
| Foot Parts | *habanshin* | 하반신 |
| Fist | *jumeok, gwon* | 주먹, 권 |
| Forefist | *ap jumeok, ap gwon* | 앞주먹, 앞권 |
| Backfist | *deung jumeok, deung gwon* | 등주먹, 등권 |
| Hammerfist | *mae jumeok, mae gwon* | 매주먹, 매권 |
| Sidefist | *yeop jumeok, yeop gwon* | 옆주먹, 옆권 |
| Underfist | *mit jumeok, mit gwon* | 밑주먹, 밑권 |
| Longfist | *gin jumeok, gin gwon* | 긴주먹, 긴권 |
| Openfist | *pyeon jumeok, pyeon gwon* | 편주먹, 편권 |
| Knucklefist | *songarak jumeok, ji gwon* | 손가락주먹, 지권 |
| Middle Knuckle Fist | *jungjijumeok, jungji gwon* | 중지주먹, 중지권 |
| Thumb Knuckle Fist | *eomjijumeok, eomji gwon* | 엄지주먹, 엄지권 |
| Fore Knuckle Fist | *injijumeok, inji gwon* | 인지주먹, 인지권 |
| Knifehand | *sonkal* | 손칼 |
| Ridgehand | *sonkal deung* | 손칼등 |
| Spear Finger | *sonkkeut* | 손끝 |
| Back of the Hand | *sondeung* | 손등 |
| Bearhand | *gomson* | 곰손 |
| Arc Hand, Crescent Hand | *bandalson* | 반달손 |
| Straight Fingertip | *seon sonkkeut* | 선손끝 |
| Upset Fingertip | *dwijibeun sonkkeut* | 뒤집은 손끝 |
| Angle Fingertip | *homi sonkkeut* | 호미 손끝 |
| Base of Knifehand | *sonkal batang* | 손칼 바탕 |
| Thumb Ridge | *eomji batang* | 엄지 바탕 |

| | | |
|---|---|---|
| Finger Belly | *songarak badak* | 손가락 바닥 |
| Finger Pincer | *sonjipge* | 손집게 |
| Palm | *sonbadak* | 손바닥 |
| Wrist | *sonmok* | 손목 |
| Forearm | *palmok* | 팔목 |
| Inner Forearm | *an palmok* | 안팔목 |
| Outer Forearm | *bakkat palmok* | 바깥팔목 |
| Back (Top) of Forearm | *deung palmok* | 등팔목 |
| Front (Bottom) of Forearm | *mit palmok* | 밑팔목 |
| Elbow | *palgup* | 팔굽 |
| Shoulder | *eokkae* | 어깨 |
| Foot | *bal* | 발 |
| Sole | *balbadak, balkkumchi* | 발바닥, 발꿈치 |
| Back Sole | *dwi kkumchi* | 뒤꿈치 |
| Ball of Foot | *apkkumchi* | 앞꿈치 |
| Front Sole, Ball of Foot | *ap balkkumchi* | 앞발꿈치 |
| Back Sole | *dwi balkkumchi* | 뒤발꿈치 |
| Toe Tip | *balkkeut* | 발끝 |
| Instep | *baldeung* | 발등 |
| Heel | *dwichuk, bal dwichuk* | 뒤축, 발뒤축 |
| Footsword | *balkal* | 발칼 |
| Knee | *mureup* | 무릎 |

# Directions

There is a slight division of the words according to style here, however as these words are so general to the language, one can't be too selective.

## WTF

| English | Romanisation | Hangeul |
|---|---|---|
| High (WF Face) | *eolgul, sangdan* | 얼굴, 상단 |
| Middle (WF Body) | *momtong, jungdan* | 몸통, 중단 |
| Low | *arae, hadan* | 아래, 하단 |
| Obverse | *baro* | 바로 |
| Reverse | *bandae* | 반대 |
| Inward | *an* | 안 |
| Outward | *bakkat* | 바깥 |

## ITF

| English | Romanisation | Hangeul |
|---|---|---|
| High Section | *nopeunde* | 높은데 |
| High | *nopi* | 높이 |
| Middle Section | *gaunde* | 가운데 |
| Middle | *gai* | 가이 |
| Low Section | *najeunde* | 낮은데 |
| Low | *naji* | 낮이 |
| Side | *yeop* | 옆 |
| Front | *ap* | 앞 |
| Back | *dwi, dwit* | 뒤, 뒷 |
| Obverse | *baro* | 바로 |
| Reverse | *bandae* | 반대 |
| Inner | *an* | 안 |

| Outer | *bakkat* | 바깥 |
| Inward | *aneuro* | 안으로 |
| Outward | *bakkeuro* | 밖으로 |
| Forward | *apeuro* | 앞으로 |
| Backward | *dwiro* | 뒤로 |
| Upward | *ollyeo* | 올려 |
| Downward | *naeryeo* | 내려 |
| From Underneath | *miteuro* | 밑으로 |
| From Above | *wiro* | 위로 |
| Across, Beyondwards | *neomeoro* | 너머로 |
| Right [adj.] | *oreun* | 오른 |
| Left [adj.] | *oen* | 왼 |
| Right Side | *oreun jjok* | 오른쪽 |
| on the Right | *oreun jjoge* | 오른쪽에 |
| Left Side | *oen jjok* | 왼쪽 |
| on the Left | *oen jjoge* | 왼쪽에 |
| Right and Left | *jwau* | 좌우 |
| Vertical | *sujik* | 수직 |
| Horizontal | *supyeong* | 수평 |
| Section (RL an idea of division into three equal parts) | *deungbun* | 등분 |
| Single | *iljung* | 일중 |
| Double | *ijung* | 이중 |
| Triple | *samjung* | 삼중 |
| Once | *hanbeon* | 한번 |
| Twice | *dubeon* | 두번 |
| Thrice | *sebeon* | 세번 |
| Many Times | *yeoreobeon* | 여러번 |

| Once More | *hanbeondeo* | 한번더 |
|---|---|---|

# Stances and Shifting

## WTF

| English | Romanisation | Hangeul |
|---|---|---|
| Stance | *seogi* | 서기 |
| Posture, Pose | *jase* | 자세 |
| Open Stance | *neolhyeo seogi* | 넓혀 서기 |
| Parallel Stance (RL Side by Side Stance) | *naranhi seogi* | 나란히 서기 |
| Right Stance | *oreun seogi* | 오른 서기 |
| Left Stance | *oen seogi* | 왼 서기 |
| Rest Stance | *pyeonhi seogi* | 편히 서기 |
| Inward Stance | *anjjong seogi* | 안쫑 서기 |
| Riding Stance | *juchum seogi* | 주춤 서기 |
| Lowered Riding Stance | *natchueo seogi* | 낮추어 서기 |
| Oblique Angle Stance | *mo seogi* | 모 서기 |
| Oblique Angle Riding Stance | *mo juchum seogi* | 모주춤 서기 |
| Inward Riding Stance | *anjjong juchum seogi* | 안쫑주춤 서기 |
| Forward Stance | *ap seogi* | 앞 서기 |
| Forward Riding Stance | *ap juchum seogi* | 앞주춤 서기 |
| Forward Inflection Stance | *apgubi seogi* | 앞굽이 서기 |
| Backward Inflection | *dwitgubi seogi* | 뒷굽이 서기 |

| Stance | | |
|---|---|---|
| T Stance | *oja seogi* | ㄱ자서기, 오자 서기 |
| Tiger Stance | *beom seogi* | 범 서기 |
| Closed Stance | *moa seogi* | 모아 서기 |
| Attention Stance | *charyeot seogi* | 차렷 서기 |
| Obverse Attention Stance | *dwichuk moa seogi* | 뒤축모아 서기 |
| Reverse Attention Stance | *apchuk moa seogi* | 앞축모아 서기 |
| Assisting Stance | *gyeotdari seogi* | 곁다리 서기 |
| Cross Stance | *kkoa seogi* | 꼬아 서기 |
| Forward Cross Stance | *apkkoa seogi* | 앞꼬아 서기 |
| Backward Cross Stance | *dwikkoa seogi* | 뒤꼬아 서기 |
| Crane Stance | *hakdari seogi* | 학다리 서기 |
| Reverse Crane Stance (PT RL Hooked Stance) | *ogeum seogi* | 오금 서기 |
| Special Poom Stance | *teuksu pum seogi* | 특수품 서기 |
| Basic Ready Stance | *gibon junbi seogi* | 기본준비 서기 |
| Fists on the Waist Read Stance | *dujumeokheori junbi seogi* | 두주먹허리준비 서기 |
| Overlapping Hands Ready Stance | *gyeopson junbi seogi* | 겹손준비 서기 |
| Covered Fist Ready Stance | *bojumeok junbi seogi* | 보주먹준비 서기 |
| Pushing Hands Ready Stance | *tongmilgi junbi seogi* | 통밀기준비 서기 |
| Sparring Stance | *gyeorugi seogi* | 겨루기 서기 |

# ITF

| English | Romanisation | Hangeul |
|---|---|---|
| Stance | *seogi* | 서기 |
| Right Stance | *oreun seogi* | 오른 서기 |
| Left Stance | *oen seogi* | 왼 서기 |
| Walking Stance | *geonneun seogi* | 걷는 서기 |
| L Stance | *nieun seogi, nieunja seogi* | ㄴ 서기, 니은 서기, ㄴ자 서기, 니은자 서기 |
| Sitting Stance | *anneun seogi* | 앉는 서기 |
| Fixed Stance | *gojeong seogi* | 고정 서기 |
| Lowered Stance | *natchwo seogi* | 낮춰 서기 |
| Closed Stance | *moa seogi* | 모아 서기 |
| Rear Foot Stance | *dwitbal seogi* | 뒷발 서기 |
| Ready Stance | *junbi seogi* | 준비 서기 |
| Bending Stance | *guburyeo seogi* | 구부러 서기 |
| Parallel Stance (RL Side by Side Stance) | *naranhi seogi* | 나란히 서기 |
| Vertical Stance | *sujik seogi* | 수직 서기 |
| Attention Stance | *charyeot seogi* | 차렷 서기 |
| Oblique Stance (CT Diagonal Stance) | *saseon seogi (daegakseon seogi)* | 사선 서기 (대각선 서기) |
| One Leg Stance | *oebal seogi* | 외발 서기 |
| X Stance (RL Intersecting Stance) | *gyocha seogi* | 교차 서기 |
| Crouched Stance | *ogeuryeo seogi* | 오그려 서기 |
| Riding Stance (CT Sitting Stance RL Horse Riding Stance) | *gima seogi* | 기마 서기 |
| Open Stance | *palja seogi* | 팔자 서기 |
| Outer Open Stance | *oepalja seogi* | 외팔자 서기 |

| Inner Open Stance | *anpalja seogi* | 안팔자 서기 |
| --- | --- | --- |
| Forward Stance (CT Walking Stance RL Anteflexion Stance) | *jeon-gul seogi* | 전굴 서기 |
| Back Stance (CT L Stance RL Retroflexion Stance) | *hugul seogi* | 후굴 서기 |
| Low Stance | *natja seogi* | 낮자 서기 |
| Heaven Hands (PT Sky Hands) | *haneulson* | 하늘손 |
| Ready Posture | *junbi jase* | 준비 자세 |
| Warrior Stance | *musa seogi* | 무사 서기 |
| Full Facing | *onmom, onhyangham* | 온몸, 온향함 |
| Half Facing | *banmom, banhyangham* | 반몸, 반향함 |
| Side Facing | *yeopmom, yeophyangham* | 옆몸, 옆향함 |
| Movement, Motion | *omgigi* | 옮기기 |
| Step | *didigi* | 디디기 |
| Moving Step | *omgyeo didigi* | 옮겨디디기 |
| Single Moving Step | *ilbo omgyeo didigi* | 일보옮겨디디기 |
| Double Moving Step | *ibo omgyeo didigi* | 이보옮겨디디기 |
| Motion Stepping | *omgyeo didimyeo* | 옮겨디디며 |
| Forward Movement | *nagagi* | 나가기 |
| Stepping Forward | *omgyeo didimyeo nagagi* | 옮겨디디며나가기 |
| Backward Movement | *deureoogi* | 들어오기 |
| Stepping Backward | *omgyeo didimyeo deureoogi* | 옮겨디디며들어오기 |
| Backward Step (RL Stand Back) | *mulleoseogi* | 물러서기 |
| Backward Stepping | *mulleoseomyeo* | 물러서며 |
| Foot Shift | *jajeunbal* | 자즌발 |

| English | Romanisation | Hangeul |
|---|---|---|
| Step Shifting | omgyeo didimyeo jajeunbal | 옮겨디디며자즌발 |
| Shift Stepping | jajeunbal omgyeo didigi | 자즌발옮겨디디기 |
| Foot Slide | mikkeureombal | 미끄럼발 |
| Slide (RL Glide) [n.] | mikkeureojigi | 미끄러지기 |
| Stepping Slide | omgyeo didimyeo mikkeureojigi | 옮겨 디디며 미끄러지기 |
| to Slide (RL to Glide) | mikkeureojida | 미끄러지다 |
| Turning | dolgi | 돌기 |
| Stationary Turning | geujari dolgi | 그자리 돌기 |
| Step Turning | omgyeo didimyeo dolgi | 옮겨디디며돌기 |
| Sliding Turn | omgyeo mikkeureojimyeo dolgi | 옮겨 미끄러지며 돌기 |

# Blocking

## WTF

| English | Romanisation | Hangeul |
|---|---|---|
| Defence | bang-eo | 방어 |
| Block | makgi | 막기 |
| Handblade Block | sonnal makgi | 손날 막기 |
| Single Handblade Block | hansonnal makgi | 한손날 막기 |
| Inner Wrist Block | an palmok makgi | 안팔목 막기 |
| Outer Wrist Block | bakkat palmok makgi | 바깥팔목 막기 |
| Back Handblade Block | sonnaldeung makgi | 손날등 막기 |
| Bent Wrist Block | guphin sonmok makgi | 굽힌손목 막기 |

| | | |
|---|---|---|
| Palmhand Block | *batangson makgi* | 바탕손 막기 |
| Hammer Fist Block | *maejumeok makgi* | 매주먹 막기 |
| Front Sole Block | *apchyeo makgi* | 앞쳐 막기 |
| Foot Blade Block | *yeopchyeo makgi* | 옆쳐 막기 |
| Foot Back Block | *bakkatchyeo makgi* | 바깥쳐 막기 |
| Shin Block | *jeonggang-i makgi* | 정강이 막기 |
| Outer Block | *bakkat makgi* | 바깥 막기 |
| Inner Block | *an makgi* | 안 막기 |
| Side Block | *yeop makgi* | 옆 막기 |
| Twisting Block | *biteureo makgi* | 비틀어 막기 |
| Assisting Block | *geodeureo makgi* | 거들어 막기 |
| Pushing Block (RL Wedging Block, Spreading Block) | *hechyeo makgi* | 헤쳐 막기 |
| Pressing Block | *nulleo makgi* | 눌러 막기 |
| Lifting Block | *chukyeo makgi* | 추켜 막기 |
| Rising Block | *ollyeo makgi* | 올려 막기 |
| Counter Block | *bada makgi* | 받아 막기 |
| Cross Block | *oetgeoreo makgi* | 엇걸어 막기 |
| Drawing Up | *kkeureo olligi* | 끌어 올리기 |
| Kicking Away Block | *chyeonae makgi* | 쳐내 막기 |
| Pushing / Deflecting Away | *geodeo naegi* | 걷어 내기 |
| Kicking Up Block | *chyeo-ollyeo makgi* | 쳐올려 막기 |
| Special Block | *teuksu makgi* | 특수 막기 |
| Scissor Block | *gawi makgi* | 가위 막기 |
| Bull Block | *hwangso makgi* | 황소 막기 |
| Diamond Block | *geumgang makgi* | 금강 막기 |
| Target Block | *pyojeok makgi* | 표적 막기 |

| English | Romanisation | Hangeul |
|---|---|---|
| Mountain Block | *santeul makgi* | 산틀 막기 |
| Single Hand Mountain Block | *oesanteul makgi* | 외산틀 막기 |
| Crane Diamond Block | *hakdari geumgang makgi* | 학다리금강 막기 |

# ITF

| English | Romanisation | Hangeul |
|---|---|---|
| Block | *makgi* | 막기 |
| Forearm Block | *palmok makgi* | 팔목 막기 |
| Knifehand Block | *sonkal makgi* | 손칼 막기 |
| Ridgehand Block | *sonkaldeung makgi* | 손칼등 막기 |
| Palm Block | *sonbadak makgi* | 손바닥 막기 |
| Arc Hand Block | *bandalson makgi* | 반달손 막기 |
| X Fist Block | *gyocha jumeok makgi* | 교차 주먹 막기 |
| Guarding Block | *daebi makgi* | 대비 막기 |
| Twin Block | *ssang makgi* | 쌍 막기 |
| Double Block | *du makgi* | 두 막기 |
| Outside Block | *bakkat makgi* | 바깥 막기 |
| Inside Block | *an makgi* | 안 막기 |
| Obverse Block | *baro makgi* | 바로 막기 |
| Reverse Block | *bandae makgi* | 반대 막기 |
| High Block | *nopeunde makgi* | 높은데 막기 |
| Middle Block | *gaunde makgi* | 가운데 막기 |
| Low Block | *najeunde makgi* | 낮은데 막기 |
| Outward Block | *bakkeuro makgi* | 밖으로 막기 |
| Inward Block | *aneuro makgi* | 안으로 막기 |
| Rising Block | *chukyeo makgi* | 추켜 막기 |

| | | |
|---|---|---|
| Circular Block | *dollyeo makgi* | 돌려 막기 |
| Upward Block | *ollyeo makgi* | 올려 막기 |
| Downward Block | *naeryeo makgi* | 내려 막기 |
| Waist Block | *heori makgi* | 허리 막기 |
| Circular Block | *dollimyeo makgi* | 돌리며 막기 |
| Wedging / Spreading Block | *hechyeo makgi* | 헤쳐 막기 |
| Pressing Block | *nulleo makgi* | 눌러 막기 |
| Pushing Block | *mireo makgi* | 밀어 막기 |
| Hooking Block (AT Extending Block) | *geolchyeo makgi* | 걸쳐 막기 |
| Scooping Block | *deureo makgi* | 들어 막기 |
| Sweeping Block | *heullyeo makgi* | 흘려 막기 |
| Checking Block | *meomchueo makgi* | 멈추어 막기 |
| Grasping Block | *butjaba makgi* | 붙잡아 막기 |
| Louring Block | *yu-in makgi* | 유인 막기 |
| Striking Block | *ttaeryeo makgi* | 때려 막기 |
| Twisting Block | *biteureo makgi* | 비틀어 막기 |
| Pulling Block | *danggyeo makgi* | 당겨 막기 |
| Dodging Block | *pihamyeo makgi* | 피하며 막기 |
| Mountain / W Block | *san makgi* | 산 막기 |
| Horizontal Block | *supyeong (RL supyeonghan) makgi* | 수평 (RL 수평한) 막기 |
| U Block | *digeut makgi, digeutja makgi* | ㄷ막기, 디귿막기, ㄷ자막기, 디귿자막기 |
| 9 Block | *guja makgi* | 구자막기 |
| Pole Block | *mongdung-i makgi* | 몽둥이 막기 |

# Kicking

# WTF

| English | Romanisation | Hangeul |
|---|---|---|
| Kick | *chagi* | 차기 |
| Front Kick | *ap chagi* | 앞 차기 |
| Side Kick | *yeop chagi* | 옆 차기 |
| Turning Kick | *dollyeo chagi* | 돌려 차기 |
| Back Kick | *dwit chagi* | 뒷 차기 |
| Hook Kick | *nakkeo chagi* | 낚어 차기 |
| Wheel Kick, Thrashing Kick | *huryeo chagi* | 후려 차기 |
| Axe Kick, Pick Down Kick | *naeryeo chagi* | 내려 차기 |
| Crescent Kick | *bandal chagi, pyojeok chagi* | 반달 차기, 표적 차기 |
| Inside Out Crescent Kick | *bandal bakkat chagi* | 반달 바깥 차기 |
| Outside In Crescent Kick | *bandal an chagi* | 반달 안 차기 |
| Turning Side Kick | *dollyeo yeop chagi* | 돌려 옆 차기 |
| Hopping Side Kick | *idan yeop chagi* | 이단 옆 차기 |
| Thrusting Kick | *chajireugi* | 차지르기 |
| Stretch Kick (PT Pushing Kick) | *chaolligi* | 차올리기 |
| Continue Kick (AT Follow-Up Kick) | *gyesokhaeseo chagi* | 계속해서 차기 |
| Crossing Kick | *bandal chagi* | 반달 차기 |
| Jump Kick | *ttwieo chagi* | 뛰어 차기 |
| Double Kick | *modumbal chagi* | 모둠발 차기 |

| English | Romanisation | Hangeul |
|---|---|---|
| Tornado Kick | *hoe-oli chagi* | 회오리 차기 |
| Scissor Kick | *gawi chagi* | 가위 차기 |
| Axe kick | *dokki chagi* | 도끼 차기 |

# ITF

| English | Romanisation | Hangeul |
|---|---|---|
| Kick | *chagi* | 차기 |
| Direction of Kicks | *cha banghyang* | 차방향 |
| Left Foot Kick | *oenbal chagi* | 왼발 차기 |
| Right Foot Kick | *oreunbal chagi* | 오른발 차기 |
| Twin Foot Kick | *ssangbal chagi* | 쌍발 차기 |
| Knee Kick | *mureup chagi* | 무릎 차기 |
| Turning Kick | *dollyeo chagi* | 돌려 차기 |
| Twisting Kick | *biteureo chagi* | 비틀어차기 |
| Crescent kick | *bandal chagi* | 반달 차기 |
| Dodging Kick (AT Evasion Kick) | *pihamyeo chagi* | 피하며 차기 |
| Horizontal Kick | *supyeong chagi* | 수평 차기 |
| Downward Kick, Axe Kick | *naeryeo chagi* | 내려 차기 |
| Vertical Kick | *sewo chagi* | 세워 차기 |
| Upward Kick | *ollyeo chagi* | 올려 차기 |
| Snapping Kick | *cha busugi* | 차부수기 |
| Piercing Kick | *cha jireugi* | 차지르기 |
| Thrusting Kick | *cha ttulgi* | 차뚫기 |
| Stamping Kick | *cha bapgi* | 차밟기 |
| Rising Kick | *cha olligi* | 차올리기 |

| | | |
|---|---|---|
| Pushing Kick | *cha milgi* | 차밀기 |
| Hooking Kick | *geolchyeo chagi* | 걸쳐 차기 |
| Punching Kick | *jireumyeo chagi* | 지르며 차기 |
| Striking Kick | *ttaerimyeo chagi* | 때리며 차기 |
| Grasping Kick | *butjaba chagi* | 붙잡아 차기 |
| Pressing Kick | *nulleo chagi* | 눌러 차기 |
| Waving Kick | *deoreo chagi* | 덜어 차기 |
| Checking Kick | *cha meomchugi* | 차멈추기 |
| Pressing Kick | *cha nureugi* | 차누르기 |
| Two-Directional Kick | *ssangbang chagi* | 쌍방 차기 |
| Consecutive Kick | *yeonsok chagi* | 연속 차기 |
| Split Kick | *ttwimyeo ssangbang chagi* | 뛰며 쌍방 차기 |
| Combination Kick | *honhap chagi* | 혼합 차기 |
| Overhead Kick (RL Jumping Beyond Kick) | *ttwieo neomeo chagi* | 뛰어 너머 차기 |
| Square Punching Kick | *sagak jireumyeo chagi* | 사각 지르며 차기 |
| Reflex Kick (RL Reflection Kick, Using Wall) | *bansa chagi* | 반사 차기 |
| Pickaxe Kick | *gokgwaeng-i chagi* | 곡괭이 차기 |
| Flying Kick | *ttwimyeo chagi* | 뛰며 차기 |
| Flying High Kick | *ttwimyeo nopi chagi* | 뛰며 높이 차기 |

# Punching

## WTF

| English | Romanisation | Hangeul |
|---|---|---|
| Punch | *jireugi* | 지르기 |
| Obverse Punch | *baro jireugi* | 바로 지르기 |
| Reverse Punch | *bandae jireugi* | 반대 지르기 |
| Vertical Fist Punch | *sewo jireugi* | 세워 지르기 |
| Inverted Fist Punch | *jeothyeo jireugi* | 젖혀 지르기 |
| Side Punch | *yeop jireugi* | 옆 지르기 |
| Downward Punch | *naeryeo jireugi* | 내려 지르기 |
| Round Punch, Spiral Punch | *dollyeo jireugi* | 돌려 지르기 |
| Upward Punch | *chi jireugi* | 치 지르기 |
| Double Inverted Fist Punch | *dujumeok jeothyeo jireugi* | 두주먹 젖혀 지르기 |
| Spring-Up Punch | *bamjumeok soseum jireugi* | 밤주먹 솟음 지르기 |
| Target Punch | *pyojeok jireugi* | 표적 지르기 |
| U Punch | *digeutja jireugi* | 디귿자 지르기 |
| Fork Punch | *chetdari jireugi* | 쳇다리 지르기 |
| Back Punch | *dwi jireugi* | 뒤 지르기 |
| Pulling Jaw Punch | *dangyeoteok jireugi* | 당겨턱 지르기 |
| Diamond Punch | *geumgang jireugi* | 금강 지르기 |
| Wing Punch | *nalgae jireugi* | 날개 지르기 |
| Strangle Punch | *kaljaebi jireugi* | 칼재비 지르기 |
| Double Punch | *dubeon jireugi* | 두번 지르기 |
| Triple Punch | *sebeon jireugi* | 세번 지르기 |

# ITF

| English | Romanisation | Hangeul |
|---|---|---|

| | | |
|---|---|---|
| Punch | *jireugi* | 지르기 |
| Forefist Punch | *ap jumeok jireugi* | 앞 주먹 지르기 |
| Vertical (PT Upright Fist) Punch | *sewo jireugi* | 세워 지르기 |
| Inverted (CT Upset Fist) Punch | *dwijibeo jumeok jireugi* | 뒤집어 주먹 지르기 |
| Knuckle Fist Punch | *jijumeok jireugi, songarakjumeok jireugi* | 지주먹 지르기, 손가락주먹 지르기 |
| Open Fist Punch | *pyeonjumeok jireugi* | 편주먹 지르기 |
| Long Fist Punch | *gin jumeok jireugi* | 긴주먹 지르기 |
| Middle Knuckle Fist Punch | *jungjijumeok jireugi* | 중지주먹 지르기 |
| Thumb Knuckle Fist Punch | *eomjijumeok jireugi* | 엄지주먹 지르기 |
| Twin Punch | *ssang jireugi* | 쌍 지르기 |
| Double Punch | *du jireugi* | 두 지르기 |
| Turning Punch | *dollyeo jireugi* | 돌려 지르기 |
| Downward Punch | *naeryeo jireugi* | 내려 지르기 |
| Upward Punch | *ollyeo jireugi* | 올려 지르기 |
| Side Punch | *yeop jireugi* | 옆 지르기 |
| Horizontal Punch | *supyeong jireugi* | 수평지르기 |
| U Punch | *digeut jireugi, digeutja jireugi* | ㄷ 지르기, ㄷ자 지르기, 디귿 지르기, 디귿자 지르기 |
| Crescent Punch | *bandal jireugi* | 반달 지르기 |
| Angle Punch (RL Grid Punch) | *gyeokja jireugi* | 격자 지르기 |

# Striking

# WTF

| English | Romanisation | Hangeul |
|---|---|---|
| Strike | chigi | 치기 |
| Hammer Fist Strike | mejumeok chigi, gakgwon chigi | 메주먹 치기, 각권 치기 |
| Knife Hand Strike | sonnal chigi, sudo chigi | 손날 치기, 수도 치기 |
| Ridge Hand Strike | sonnaldeung chigi | 손날등 치기 |
| Bear Hand Strike | gomson chigi | 곰손 치기 |
| Palm Heel Strike | batangson chigi, janggwon chigi | 바탕손 치기, 장권 치기 |
| Arc Hand Strike | agwison chigi | 아귀손 치기 |
| Bent Wrist Strike | guphinsonmok chigi | 굽힌손목 치기 |
| Pincer Fist Strike | jipge chigi | 집게 치기 |
| Elbow Strike | palgup chigi | 팔굽 치기 |
| Knee Strike | mureup chigi | 무릎 치기 |
| Back Fist Strike | igwon chigi, deung jumeok chigi | 이권 치기, 등주먹 치기 |
| Back Hand Strike | sondeung chigi | 손등 치기 |
| Turning Strike | dollyeo chigi | 돌려 치기 |
| Upward Strike | ollyeo chigi | 올려 치기 |
| Downward Strike | naeryeo chigi | 내려 치기 |
| Backward Strike | dwiro chigi | 뒤로 치기 |
| Assisted Strike | geodeureo chigi | 거들어 치기 |
| Target Strike | pyojeok chigi | 표적 치기 |
| Strangle Strike | kaljaebi chigi | 칼재비 치기 |
| Jaw Strike | jebi pum teok chigi | 제비품 턱 치기 |
| Neck Strike | jebi pum mok chigi | 제비품 목 치기 |
| Pulling Jaw Strike | danggyeo teok chigi | 당겨 턱 치기 |

| Yoke Strike | *meong-e chigi* | 멍에치기 |
| Flank Strike | *yeopguri chigi* | 옆구리치기 |
| Double Bladehand Strike | *dusonnal chigi* | 두손날치기 |
| Single Bladehand Twisting Strike | *biteureo hansonnal chigi* | 비틀어 한손날 치기 |

## ITF

| English | Romanisation | Hangeul |
| --- | --- | --- |
| Strike, Thrash | *ttaerigi* | 때리기 |
| Single Strike | *oe ttaerigi* | 외 때리기 |
| Twin Strike | *ssang ttaerigi* | 쌍 때리기 |
| Knifehand Strike | *sonkal ttaerigi* | 손칼 때리기 |
| Elbow Strike | *palgup ttaerigi* | 팔굽 때리기 |
| Ridgehand Strike | *sonkaldeung ttaerigi* | 손칼등 때리기 |
| Backfist Strike | *deungjumeok ttaerigi* | 등주먹 때리기 |
| Archand Strike | *bandalson ttaerigi* | 반달손 때리기 |
| Bearhand Strike | *gomson ttaerigi* | 곰손 때리기 |
| Underfist Strike | *mitjumeok ttaerigi* | 밑주먹 때리기 |
| Back Hand Strike | *sondeung ttaerigi* | 손등 때리기 |
| Sidefist Strike | *yeopjumeok ttaerigi* | 옆주먹 때리기 |
| Upper Elbow Strike | *wipalgup ttaerigi* | 위팔굽 때리기 |
| Horizontal Strike | *supyeong ttaerigi* | 수평 때리기 |

# Thrusting

As thrusts aren't a particularly in-depth part of most syllabuses, and in an attempt to reduce unnecessary repetition in this index, many of the words that you may use for thrusting techniques are to be found in other sections.

Thrusting techniques also tend to follow a division in terms of terminology between the two main styles. As always, the first table here contains World Federation words, and the second contains those for the International Federation.

# WTF

| English | Romanisation | Hangeul |
|---|---|---|
| Thrust | *jjireugi* | 찌르기 |
| Spear Hand Strike | *pyeonsonkkeut jjireugi, gwansu jjireugi* | 편손끝 찌르기, 관수 찌르기 |
| Spear Hand Strike {Palm to Side} | *pyeonsonkkeut sewo jjireugi* | 편손끝세워 찌르기 |
| Spear Hand Strike {Palm Down} | *pyeonsonkkeut eoppeo jjireugi* | 편손끝 엎퍼 찌르기 |
| Spear Hand Strike {Palm Up} | *pyeonsonkkeut jechyeo jjireugi* | 편손끝제처 찌르기 |
| One Finger Strike | *hansonkkeut jjireugi* | 한손끝 찌르기 |
| Two Finger Strike {Together} | *mo-eundusonkkeut jjireugi* | 모은두손끝 찌르기 |
| Two Finger Strike {Separate} | *gawison jjireugi* | 가위손 찌르기 |
| Three Finger Strike | *mo-eunsesonkkeut jjireugi* | 모은세손끝 찌르기 |

# ITF

| English | Romanisation | Hangeul |
|---|---|---|
| Thrust | *ttulgi* | 뚫기 |

| | | |
|---|---|---|
| Single Thrust | *oe ttulgi* | 외 뚫기 |
| Twin Thrust | *ssang ttulgi* | 쌍 뚫기 |
| Double Thrust | *du ttulgi* | 두 뚫기 |
| Finger Thrust | *songarak ttulgi* | 손가락 뚫기 |
| Fingertip Thrust | *sonkkeut ttulgi* | 손끝 뚫기 |
| Elbow Thrust | *palgup ttulgi* | 팔굽 뚫기 |
| Straight Thrust | *seon ttulgi* | 선 뚫기 |
| Upset Thrust | *dwijibeun ttulgi* | 뒤집은 뚫기 |
| Angle Thrust | *homi ttulgi* | 호미뚫기 |

# Grasping and Releasing

| English | Romanisation | Hangeul |
|---|---|---|
| Grasp (RL Catch) | *japgi* | 잡기 |
| | *butjapgi* | 붙잡기 |
| Grasping (RL Catching) | *jaba* | 잡아 |
| | *butjaba* | 붙잡아 |
| Pull | *kkeulgi* | 끌기 |
| Archand Forearm Grasp | *agwison palmok japgi* | 아귀손 팔목 잡기 |
| Wrist Grasp | *sonmok japgi* | 손목 잡기 |
| Forearm Twisting Grasping Pull | *palmok biteureo jaba kkeulgi* | 팔목 비틀어 잡아 끌기 |
| Ankle Grasp | *balmok japgi* | 발목 잡기 |
| Head Grasp | *meori japgi* | 머리 잡기 |
| Shoulder Grasp | *eokkae japgi* | 어깨 잡기 |
| Neck Grasp | *mok japgi* | 목 잡기 |
| Pincer Hand Grasp | *jipgeson japgi* | 집게손 잡기 |

| English | Romanisation | Hangeul |
|---|---|---|
| U Grasp | *digeutja japgi* | 디귿자 잡기 |
| Pole Grasp | *mongdung-i japgi* | 몽둥이 잡기 |
| Release, Retraction | *ppaegi* | 빼기 |
| Release Movement | *ja pyeosseul ttae* | 자 벼쓸 때 |
| Lock Release, Hold Release | *meong-e ppaegi* | 멍에 빼기 |
| Underneath Release | *miteuro ppaegi* | 밑으로 빼기 |
| Upward Release | *wiro ppaegi* | 위로 빼기 |

# Other Techniques

| English | Romanisation | Hangeul |
|---|---|---|
| Ground | *ttang* | 땅 |
| on the Ground, from the Ground | *hyeonjang-eseo* | 현장에서 |
| Ground (PT From the Ground RL Lying Down) | *nuwo* | 누워 |
| Jump | *ttwigi* | 뛰기 |
| Flying (RL Jumping) | *ttwieo* | 뛰어 |
| Flying (RL Jumping) | *ttwimyeo* | 뛰며 |
| Press | *nureugi* | 누르기 |
| Dodge | *pihagi* | 피하기 |
| Catch, Hold, Grab | *bundeulgi* | 붙들기 |
| Body Drop | *mom natchugi* | 몸 낮추기 |
| Hold | *batchigi* | 받치기 |
| Check | *meomchugi* | 멈추기 |
| Cover | *garigi* | 가리기 |

# Weapons

Whilst weapons are not used in Taekwondo, some movement names contain the names of weapons, which they may defend against or represent. You may need to describe a movement to deal with a particular weapon. It is also arguably important to know more than just what one's own martial art includes.

| English | Romanisation | Hangeul |
| --- | --- | --- |
| Weapons | *mugi* | 무기 |
| Cane | *jipang-i* | 지팡이 |
| Short Stick | *danbong* | 단봉 |
| Middle Staff | *jungbong* | 중봉 |
| Long Staff | *jangbong* | 장봉 |
| Knife | *kal* | 칼 |
| Dagger | *dando* | 단도 |
| Sword | *geom* | 검 |
| Handle | *jaru* | 자루 |
| Spear | *chang* | 창 |
| Fan | *buchae* | 부채 |
| Rope | *jul, batjul* | 줄, 밧줄 |
| Bayonet | *chonggeom* | 총검 |
| Pole | *mongdung-i* | 몽둥이 |
| Club | *gonbong* | 곤봉 |
| Pistol | *gwonchong* | 권총 |

# Titles and Honorifics

# Titles

Titles in Korean can a lot of the time be the job or position that a person has. In Korean, one can simply address someone by their title.

| English | Romanisation | Hangeul | Hanja |
|---|---|---|---|
| Title | *chingho* | 칭호 | 稱號 |
| Capacity, Skill, Faculty, Function, Position, Job | *gineung* | 기능 | 技能, 機能 |
| Master (RL Controller) | *gwanjang nim* | 관장님 | |
| Chief Instructor | *jangsa nim* | 장사님 | |
| Instructor | *sabeom nim* | 사범님 | |
| Teacher | *gyosa nim* | 교사님 | 教師 |
| Assistant Teacher | *jogyo nim* | 조교님 | 助教 |
| Assistant Instructor, Substitute Instructor (RL Vice Instructor) | *busabeom nim* | 부사범님 | |
| Student Teacher, Trainee Teacher | *gyosaeng nim* | 교생님 | 教生 |
| Senior Student | *seonbae* | 선배 | 先輩 |
| Junior Student | *hubae* | 후배 | 後輩 |
| Student (WA Disciples) | *jeja* | 제자 | 弟子 |
| Expert | *sungnyeonja* | 숙련자 | |
| Leader | *jidoja* | 지도자 | 指導者 |
| Parents | *bumo nim* | 부모님 | 父母 |
| Grandparents | *jobumo nim* | 조부모님 | 祖父母 |
| President | *chongjae* | 총재 | 總裁 |
| Ambassador | *daesa* | 대사 | |
| Teacher | *seonsaeng* | 선생 | 先生 |

| Student | *haksaeng* | 학생 | 學生 |
| Warrior | *jeonsa, musa* | 전사, 무사 | 戰士 |
| School Headteacher | *gyojang* | 교장 | 校長 |

# Honorifics

Honorifics are suffixes that are attached to titles or names in order to reflect the status of the person being addressed. All are used when talking to or about the person. This is another example of how the Korean language is built around status and merit.

| English | Application | Romanisation | Hangeul | Hanja |
|---|---|---|---|---|
| Honorifics | | *nopimmal* | 높임말 | |
| Honorifics | | *gyeong-eo* | 경어 | 敬語 |
| Extremely Formal: for monarchs or presidents. | | *gwiha, gakha* | 귀하, 각하 | 貴下, 閣下 |
| Formal: occasions such as weddings, male only. | After full or last name. | *gun* | 군 | 君 |
| Formal: occasions such as weddings, female only. | After full or last name. | *yang* | 양 | 孃 |
| Formal: general occasions, used often in martial arts. | After title or full name. | *nim* | 님 | |
| Senior Student | Used alone or as a title. | *seonbae* | 선배 | 先輩 |

| Junior Student | Used alone or as a title. | hubae | 후배 | 後輩 |
| Informal: meaning mentor or "one who has lived before" | After full or last name. | seonsaeng | 선생 | 先生 |
| Informal: equal status. | After full or first name; never after just last name. | sshi | 씨 | 氏 |

# Salutations

This section is far more advanced in terms of Korean grammar. For the purposes of Korean language in Taekwondo, just the phrases have been listed, rather than a demonstration of the grammatical points.

| English | Romanisation | Hangeul |
|---|---|---|
| Salutation [n. & excl.] {Often Bowing} | insa | 인사 |
| Hello | annyeong haseyo | 안녕 하세요 |
| Goodbye {to one who is leaving} | annyeonghi gaseyo | 안녕 히 가세요 |
| Goodbye {to one who is staying} | annyeonghi gyeseyo | 안녕 히 계세요 |
| Thank you | gamsa hamnida | 감사 합니다 |
| You're welcome | cheonmaneyo | 천만에요 |
| Sorry | joesong hamnida | 죄송합니다 |
| Excuse me {On leaving, entering, or interrupting} | shillye hamnida | 실례합니다 |
| Excuse me {For | shillye haesseumnida | 실례했음니다 |

| | | |
|---|---|---|
| something that you have done} | | |
| Excuse me {For something that you will do} | *shillye hagesseumnida* | 실례하겠음니다 |
| Good Luck | *haeng-uneul bilgesseoyo* | 행운을 빌겠어요 |
| Congratulations [excl.] | *chukha* | 축하 |
| Good luck | *haeng-uneul bimnida* | 행운을 빕니다 |
| Yes | *ne* | 네 |
| No | *aniyo* | 아니요 |

# Commands

## Simple Commands

There are two ways of saying commands in Taekwondo in Korean. Mostly people will use simple commands; these correspond to the first table in this section.

The simple commands are not normal command phrases or sentences; they are mostly nouns or exclamations. There are many commands in this first list which are commonplace in Korean speech and would be perfectly understood by a native speaker. There are other commands which are just nouns that imply the command.

| English | Romanisation | Hangeul |
|---|---|---|
| Commands | *guryeong* | 구령 |
| Attention [excl.] | *charyeo* | 차려 |
| Bow | *gyeongnye* | 경례 |
| Bow to Instructor | *sabeomnim kke gyeongnye* | 사범님께경례 |

| | | |
|---|---|---|
| Bow to Flag | *gukgi edae hayeo kyeongnye* | 국기에대 하여 경례 |
| At Ease | *swieo* | 쉬어 |
| Continue | *gyesok* | 계속 |
| Adjust Uniform | *dobok jeongni* | 도복 정리 |
| Sit for Meditation | *anjeo mungnyeom* | 앉어 묵념 |
| As You Were [excl.] | *baro* | 바로 |
| Dismiss | *haesan* | 해산 |
| Rest | *hyushik* | 휴식 |
| About Turn | *dwiro dora* | 뒤로돌아 |
| Right and Left Face | *jwau hyang-u* | 좌우향우 |
| Ready, Prepare | *junbi* | 준비 |
| Begin | *shijak* | 시작 |
| Stop [excl.] | *geuman* | 그만 |
| Switch Feet | *balbakkoe* | 발바꿔 |

## Complex Commands

There are some commands that cannot be said as the noun or exclamation construction. Sometimes this is because the meaning would then be too general, and one wouldn't know what the speaker intends.

Full command phrases have the advantage of being much more specific and so we can interpret them more easily, hence there is a greater range of complex commands. The disadvantage is that they add length, making them less convenient to say, though in some cases they are the only construction available.

| English | Romanisation | Hangeul |
|---|---|---|
| Stand to Attention | *charyeo jasereul chwihashipshiyo* | 차려 자세를 취하십시요 |
| | *charyeo jasereul* | 차려 자세를 서십시요 |

|  | seoshipshiyo |  |
|---|---|---|
| Stand at Ease | swieo jasereul chwihashipshiyo | 쉬어 자세로 취하십시요 |
|  | swieo jasereul seoshipshiyo | 쉬어 자세로 서십시요 |
| Bow | gyeongnye hashipshiyo | 경례 하십시요 |
| Bow to Instructor | sabeomnimkke gyeongnye hashipshiyo | 사범님께 경례 하십시요 |
| Sit Down | anjeu shipshiyo | 앉으십시요 |
| Sit for Meditation | mungnyeomeulwihan anjeu shipshiyo | 묵념을위한 앉으십시요 |
| Stand Up | seo shipshiyo | 서십시요 |
| Line Up | julseo shipshiyo | 줄서십시요 |
| Dismiss | haesan hashipshiyo | 해산 하십시요 |
| Rest | hyushik hashipshiyo | 휴식 하십시요 |
| Adjust Uniform | dobok jeongnihashipshiyo | 도복 정리하십시요 |
|  | gyobok jeongnihashipshiyo | 교복 정리하십시요 |
| Ready, Prepare | junbi hashipshiyo | 준비 하십시요 |
| Begin, Start | shijak hashipshiyo | 시작 하십시요 |
| Stop | geumandu shipshiyo | 그만두십시요 |
| Separate | gallishipshiyo | 갈리십시요 |
| Continue | gyesok hashipshiyo | 계속 하십시요 |
| Switch Feet | bal bakkushipshiyo | 발 바꾸십시요 |
| Switch Hands | son bakkushipshiyo | 손 바꾸십시요 |
| Switch Stance | seogi bakkushipshiyo | 서기 바꾸십시요 |
| My Timing | naui shigireul matchugi | 나의 시기를 맞추기 |
| Your Timing | neohuideurui shigireul matchugi | 너희들의 시기를 맞추기 |

# Related Vocabulary

This last section throws together the remaining words and phrases that you may find useful. Some entries in the following tables clear up ambiguous aspects to entries in other sections; others are grammatically based and are useful in compound phrases.

| English | Romanisation | Hangeul | Hanja |
|---|---|---|---|
| Time | *shigi* | 시기 | |
| Timing | *shigireul matchugi* | 시기를 맞추기 | |
| Pace, Speed, Rate | *sokdo* | 속도 | |
| Timing | *sokdojojeol* | 속도조절 | |
| For {Purpose} | *eulwihan, reulwihan* | 을위한, 를위한 | |
| To, For {a Person} | *kke* | 께 | |
| of | *ui* | 의 | |
| And [joining nouns] | *wa / gwa* | 와 / 과 | |
| And [joining adjectives] | *go* | 고 | |
| And [joining verbs] | *hago* | 하고 | |
| Then | *geurigo* | 그리고 | |
| to Alternate | *gyochehada* | 교체하다 | |
| to Grasp, to Clench | *butjapda* | 붙잡다 | |
| to Catch, to Seize, to Grasp | *japda* | 잡다 | |
| Parallel [adj.] | *pyeonghaengseon, pyeonghaenghaneun* | 평행선, 평행하는 | |
| the Great King | *daewang* | 대왕 | 大王 |
| Long | *gin* | 긴 | |

| Short | *jjalbeun* | 짧은 |
|---|---|---|

# Forming Movement Names

The information listed in this index tries to be non-repetitive, that is individual words are given, with the hope that you can effortlessly piece them together to create the movement names for whatever syllabus you are studying. Nevertheless, there are some ideas that are important to remember when creating the full movement names yourself.

Firstly, a movement is a single concept, it is one thing, and as such it is one noun. There can only be one noun in the name of a movement, otherwise the name is ambiguous. People often try to put two nouns together; this instead just lists actions rather than describes them.

| (RL Rise Block) | *olligi makgi* | 올리기 막기 | Incorrect |
|---|---|---|---|
| Rising Block | *ollyeo makgi* | 올려 막기 | Correct |

As long as you use the adjective form of a word, you can have as many as you like describing the movement, though obviously don't use words of opposite meaning just to create hypothetical movements, which has been done. The following example has two contradictory terms, this movement is not possible, and sometimes people try to make extra terms by just throwing words together. Clearly here, it doesn't work.

| (RL Back Side Strike) | *dwiyeop ttaerigi* | 뒤옆 때리기 | Incorrect |
|---|---|---|---|

The entries are listed in blocks, often according to groups of similar attributes. For movement terms, each word is given alongside the action noun. You should be able to strip away the key word or phrase from each one, and then place them in front of one noun to make a full movement name.

| Knifehand Block | *sonkal makgi* | 손칼 막기 |
|---|---|---|
| Obverse Block | *baro makgi* | 바로 막기 |
| Striking Block | *ttaeryeo makgi* | 때려 막기 |

| Obverse Knifehand Striking Block | baro sonkal ttaeryeo makgi | 바로 손칼 때려 막기 |
|---|---|---|

The entire index is designed for you to be able to do this. On a similar point, in some cases you may want to bring together two different ideas, for which both the terminology is given as a noun. In this instance, you must change one of them into an adjective.

| Forwards Motion | apeuro gagi | 앞으로 가기 | Correct |
|---|---|---|---|
| Obverse Punch | baro jireugi | 바로 지르기 | Correct |
| (RL Forward Motion Obverse Punch) | apeuro gagi baro jireugi | 앞으로 가기 바로 지르기 | Incorrect |
| Forward Obverse Punch | apeuro baro jireugi | 앞으로 바로 지르기 | Correct |

Should you wish to describe two different movements that are happening at the same time however, then you again do not use the incorrect formation just mentioned, but you use the special suffix mentioned in the suffixes section.

| (RL Punching Kick) | jilleo chagi | 질러 차기 | Incorrect |
|---|---|---|---|
| Punch whilst Kicking (Simultaneous Movements) | jireumyeo chagi | 지르며 차기 | Correct |

Many syllabuses will also have movements that consist of several techniques following on from one another. Combinations of movements should be listed in order as a list, they are not simultaneous movements, and therefore you cannot use the previous suffix.

| (RL Punch whilst Kicking) | jireumyeo chagi | 지르며 차기 | Incorrect |
|---|---|---|---|
| Punch then Kick | jireugi geurigo chagi | 지르기 그리고 차기 | Correct |

# ⑤ 대화과사용

# Conversation and Usage

# In Lessons

The amount of Korean language used in Taekwondo lessons will vary greatly from club to club. It is normally dependant on the eagerness of the students to actually learn and then practise speaking it, which can sometimes be a direct result of the instructor's enthusiasm. Nevertheless, here is some general advice for the inclusion of the language into training time.

Mainly it is important whenever you name a movement in English, to then name it in Korean. There are several important reasons for this. Firstly, it is good memory practise, both for you and the person you are talking to. You may not have learnt the exact phrasing of the movement and therefore may have to think about how to construct the term. Secondly and similarly, the language is often a dominating aspect of the theory in Taekwondo organisations, and as some students will be more reluctant or less motivated to learn it independently, by speaking Korean you are incidentally helping those students learn part of the syllabus. Thirdly, some movements have multiple English names, hence by naming it in two languages, you reduce ambiguity.

As you progress through the ranks, you are generally expected to show a higher commitment and knowledge. Hence it would be appropriate to use greetings and short conversational phrases when possible to talk to other students of similar or higher grade. At higher grades also, you are quite likely to teach other students or perhaps take the class momentarily, such is the way of martial arts. In this sort of situation, Korean commands ought to be used.

# Out of Lessons

At any events that occur within the organisation or the world of Taekwondo, such as examinations or competitions, you have an excellent opportunity to use not only Hangeul, but Hanja also. At these sorts of events, a higher degree of formality is common; as such the older language can be very interesting. In this book, Hanja has been listed principally to those words which could be used at events.

In a situation away from both lessons and events completely, if you happen to meet a fellow student, instructor, or even master, on the bus or in the street for example, some people like to behave as they would if they were in the Taekwondo context, and others prefer to act as they would with any other member of society.

I would say that one should communicate and present the same attitude around fellow practitioners when inside and outside the martial art. Of course this is your choice whether you behave this way; there is nothing to make you do this, but then there is nothing to make you act accordingly in lessons either, apart from the instructor perhaps banning you from the class. So therefore it is the same reasons that compel you to behave accordingly in lessons which ought to compel you to behave in the same way outside of them.

There is the question of respect. This respect should not end when outside the doors of the training hall. Nothing has changed, your instructor is still superior and well accomplished in Taekwondo and for that deserves the same level of respect. This is of course shown through bowing and communicating in Korean when possible. Indeed by deliberately not behaving in the same way, you are effectively conveying that you do not recognise this person's achievements.

Taekwondo is also of course, not just something you do for one hour two evenings a week, or however often you attend it. Taekwondo should affect all aspects of your life. Otherwise are the morals that guide your usage of the skills within lessons still present in real situations? If the attitude you present to Taekwondo is only present during lessons and other events, is it really worth having that attitude at all?

By dropping the behaviour out of the Taekwondo context, it also suggests that you see it as some fantasy; like something from a film. This of course, would be offensive to anyone of Korean culture.

# 결말

# ⑥ Conclusion

# Examples of Mistakes

In this brief section, I have emphasised some of the instances of when terminology goes wrong. This is just some of what has been found when scouring sources which is not only completely incorrect, but the meaning instead has turned up slightly amusing. Unfortunately it cannot be noted where these have been found, although this is largely irrelevant as there are many lists which contain these particular examples. Almost every vocabulary list has something of this nature.

| Walking Punch | *beondae jireugi* | 번대지르기 |

This is a very typical example of how such a seemingly small change can change the intended meaning entirely, this does not mean *walking punch* in the slightest, but *time punch*. You can find the actual translation for this entry in this book.

| Bow to the flag | *kuk gi bay ray* |

Most sources have no characters to back them up, because learning the symbols requires a lot more effort, so just the attempted phonetic pronunciation is given. In this example the word for *flag* is arguably correct, but where this word for *bow* came from is a mystery.

| Line Up | *annoda wie* |
| Stand Up | *ye ru sut* |
| On My Count | *ku ryung ee mat cho so* |

It is most likely that these are phrases which have been either made up or very badly translated and romanised. The result is completely uninterpretable and useless.

| Right About Face | *orun diro dora* |

One can just about discern real words from this, but it has clearly just been thrown together, as a method for making new commands, without real consideration for what each word actually means. In this case, one is saying to turn both to the right and behind, rather than turn to the right.

This is why it is important to understand the type of word you are using and its construction, before you make compound phrases.

| Fixed Stance | *gojang seogi* | 고장서기 |

The accurate translation of this was explained earlier on. This here means *breakdown stance*, a word normally used for referring to a vehicle. The actual word admittedly is similar, but again this is a fine example of how even variations that we perceive as slight can change the actual meaning entirely.

| One Leg Stance | *wae bal sogi* |

This is an overwhelmingly common mistake, instead of meaning *one leg stance*, this phrase actually means *why leg stance*. You may remember that the two sounds involved here, "*wae*" the incorrect one and "*oe*" the correct one, are pronounced almost identically, but their written form is quite different, hence changing the meaning.

And finally, I do not wish to create stereotypes, but a lot of the terminology from American websites is utterly wrong, not all or most of it, but a lot. This is largely because whilst the whole martial art has undergone the process of separation several times on an international level, it has happened even more in America. There are now a lot of small groups of local clubs in America, and as such the terminology has become decreasingly accurate. This terminology has then found its way onto hobby websites.

# About the Author

When I started Taekwondo I took my first grading very quickly. It is debatable that it was too early, as I did not at all know what I was doing. Despite this though, I did pass, and it may have been the events at this first grading which ultimately lead to me writing this book.

In the organisation I'm in, which is the Taekwondo Association of Great Britain, our gradings consist of two parts: the main group practical sessions which are marked by a very senior visiting member, and then individual theoretical sessions marked by black belt students from local clubs.

These assistant black belts however aren't allowed any books to ask the questions from, they just have to remember everything in the syllabus and think of questions on the spot. This is a perfectly reasonable expectation, but it is rarely achieved. The theory examiners seldom ask questions appropriate to the grade of the student because they cannot remember the exact syllabus.

You can imagine that for higher belts this would be fine, because quite often they just ask quite easy questions that they think may catch the applicants out. Conversely I was most unfortunate, as a new member, to be asked questions that were above my grade, by about one or two levels. This had annoyed me greatly, as I had memorised all the information that I was supposed to. After the grading therefore, I had resolved to always learn the theory of the grade above and sometimes even further, so as not to be caught out again. Ironically I then only got easy questions.

There are then several simultaneous projects and events that happened over the course of a few years. Firstly, because I obsessed over the terminology thereafter I became thoroughly proficient at the Korean terminology. As a competitive person I made it my goal to know the material we were given inside out. Bearing in mind that the terminology we were given to learn was not as accurate as that presented in this book.

Secondly, I received many books on Taekwondo as gifts, and purchased some myself. These were mainstream books that barely scratched the surface, and as such the terminology in them was appalling, and interestingly totally different from what I had learnt. I brushed this difference aside by deciding that what I had learnt must have correct.

Thirdly, as a purely interest project, I wrote a booklet on the first pattern and printed it out. My older brother, who does not do Taekwondo, believed it to be an excellent product, and convinced me to print more and sell them over the internet. I then over the years proceeded to make many similar items for sale.

A couple of years before writing the book I had been learning Chinese, and had completed a couple of qualifications in it. As I had several products for martial arts other than Taekwondo, it made sense for me to make a product which could exercise that knowledge. I started making a database of Chinese martial arts terminology, in particular modern Wushu.

I then later started learning Korean in full as well. This all culminated and I decided to halt work on the Chinese vocabulary, because it took a lot longer than I had expected due to Chinese being rather a tricky language, and started work on a similar database for Korean terminology in my own martial art.

# Writing the Book

So there were several causes for why I decided to start the book. I had seen hundreds of terminology lists over the years and was now fed up with the discrepancies between sources, wondering just which one, if any, was right. It also fuelled my desire for a greater knowledge on the subject.

The crucial starting point for the book was that I found one website, in the backwaters of the internet, which had not only the Romanisation of the Korean on it, but the actual Korean as well. I thought that this was brilliant, somewhere which actually had evidence for the terminology it was claiming to be correct. Later it turned out that many of them were wrong, but it was the kick-start that the process needed. The downside was that there were only a fraction of the necessary words. A fraction which when compared to the database here is minute.

The remedy for this was to gather information from the sources which did not have the full Korean listed and then find out what it was. I looked through the syllabuses of countless clubs and organisations and found out which words they were trying to use.

I started to sort all of the entries that I found into a database. The techniques for doing this became ever more complex; if there is a decent English to Korean translator on the English internet, it is well hidden.

Due to the techniques I was using to verify that each word was correct, it also seemed that every time I would have confirmation of one word, another word would be provided with it which had no such confirmation. This lead to a rapid expansion of the database, and as such, the number of words listed here far exceeds the number of words most organisations have access to.

Eventually however, it got to a point where there were almost no more useful words to find, and the now huge database was finished. Due to all of this, this book not only contains the most English to Korean terminology out of all sources across the world, but this is the most accurate source.

There are still a few words which are left on the original database and have not been printed in this book. Some words it seems, are just impossible to track down, nothing seems to confirm that they are actually Korean words, yet so many organisations claim that they are. If this book is revised then hopefully these last few words will make it in.

Whilst I myself was capable of using the information that I had found, for the ordinary practitioner the terminology, even in romanised form, wasn't necessarily as useful as the original sources which I had looked at to find out which words are needed. This is because despite the best efforts of the scholars who developed the revised romanisation system, it is still not completely interpretable by westerners, who are used to just five vowels. This meant that I had to write sections in the book which could allow the reader to develop their language skills up to that which is necessary to interpret the data. This resulted ultimately in a large language skills section, which desperately tries to cram in all the necessary information.

I then decided to add many other sections to the book in an attempt to give a well rounded course. This included explaining just why this information is important, which is emphasised in numerous ways, and delving into all the nuances of the language so that all questions are answered. Hopefully the result is a book which can give a Taekwondo practitioner all the information they will ever need about the terminology and language of Taekwondo.

# Copyright ©

## Reminder Notice

This book and audio disc are classed as intellectual property, and as such, is protected by full copyright. The copyright of this book and compact disc is the property of its author. A summary of copyright rules and laws are listed below. This summary does not represent all the laws of copyright, but acts as a reminder.

You may only copy a work protected by copyright with the copyright owner's written permission. For this book and all its contents, and for the audio disc and all its contents, the copyright owner is its author Benjamin T. Milnes.

Copyright applies to any medium. This means that you may not reproduce this work in another or the same medium without permission. The contents of this book or the CD may not be reproduced materially as a book, poster, or any other format. The information may not be reproduced or stored electronically, including being displayed on a website, or used as a shared resource, or any other format. You may not publically display this book or the information contained within it in any format.

Copyright applies to individuals and groups. You may not as an individual break any of the laws of copyright by replicating the work for fellow students, friends, or family, and you are still open to prosecution if you act under the name of an organisation. Organisations may not decide to collectively breach the laws of copyright either.

Copyright is an international agreement. It doesn't matter where you are; if you break the rules of copyright you are open to prosecution.

An important reason not to replicate this work, is simply because its accuracy will be lost through the copying process, which when it comes to this subject is unacceptable. The reason terminology has such low standards at the moment, is due to inaccuracy; therefore it is unacceptable to further repeat the process.

# Special Notice

This is all applied under copyright, however I should like to remind you that no organisation may copy the information contained within this book or on the compact disc for use as curriculum material without express permission from the copyright owner. Should you wish to approve the book and CD for use in your organisation or set it specifically as a course book, it would be prudent to contact the copyright owner.

# Audio CD Tracks

Depending on the source which you acquired this book from, it may or may not have the Audio CD with it. If you do not have the CD, it is available online from various major sources. Depending on your learning style, you may find it more or less beneficial for actually memorising the words in the index, but it is very important for learning how to pronounce the words correctly.

The CD matches up to many of the sections in the book.

| | | |
|---|---|---|
| ① | **INTRODUCTION** | 1 |
| ② | **LANGUAGE SKILLS AND CONCEPTS** | 2, 3 - 5 |
| | SOUNDS AND PRONUNCIATION | 3 |
| | VOWELS * | 4 |
| | CONSONANTS * | 5 |
| ③ | **TERMINOLOGY AND PHRASES** | 6, 7 - 33 |
| | NUMBERS AND COUNTING * | 7 |
| | GENERAL VOCABULARY * | 8 |
| | CLOTHING, TRAINING AND LESSONS * | 9 |
| | FORMS * | 10 |
| | SPARRING * | 11 |
| | COMPETITIONS AND EXAMINATIONS * | 12 |
| | EQUIPMENT * | 13 |
| | VIRTUES AND MORALITY * | 14 |
| | ACTIONS ** | 15 |

| | |
|---|---|
| BODY PARTS AND CRITICAL POINTS * | 16 |
| STRIKING SURFACES AND HAND FORMATIONS * | 17 |
| DIRECTIONS * | 18 |
| STANCES AND SHIFTING * | 19 |
| BLOCKING * | 20 |
| KICKING * | 21 |
| PUNCHING * | 22 |
| STRIKING * | 23 |
| THRUSTING * | 24 |
| GRASPING AND RELEASING * | 25 |
| OTHER TECHNIQUES * | 26 |
| WEAPONS ** | 27 |
| TITLES AND HONOURIFICS *** | 28 |
| SALUTATIONS *** | 29 |
| COMMANDS * | 30 |
| RELATED VOCABULARY *** | 31 |
| FORMING MOVEMENT NAMES *** | 32 |
| ④ CONCLUSION AND TEST | 33, 34 - 43 |
| TEST LEVEL ONE | 34 |
| TEST LEVEL TWO | 35 |
| TEST LEVEL THREE | 36 |
| TEST LEVEL FOUR | 37 |

| | |
|---|---|
| TEST LEVEL FIVE | 38 |
| TEST LEVEL SIX | 39 |
| TEST LEVEL SEVEN | 40 |
| TEST LEVEL EIGHT | 41 |
| TEST LEVEL NINE | 42 |
| TEST LEVEL TEN | 43 |

# Notes

# Notes

# Notes

# Notes

Made in the USA
Lexington, KY
29 March 2013